Gluten Sugar Dairy Free
Big Book of Recipes
VOLUME I

Michelle E. DeBerge

Copyright © 2015 Michelle E. DeBerge
All rights reserved.
ISBN-10:151958802X
ISBN-13: 978-1519588029

Dedication

I dedicate this book to all of the amazing people in the GSDF Community, our private FaceBook support group and for all the graduates of the GSDF 8-part Basics Course. These people have touched my heart in so many ways. As they learned to cook and live gluten, sugar, dairy free for medical and health reasons. I watched them get some of their independence back as they learned prep secrets and easy recipes. I heard from others as they began to get some of their health back, their hope back and most of all, not feel alone and confused again. Every day I watch them bravely try new ingredients, recipes or ways of doing things and I have the honor to witness their lives transform.

I dedicate this book to those that have felt overwhelmed, alone, frustrated and in physical pain due to food allergies or other medical illnesses that have you eating without gluten, sugar and dairy.

Our community at Gluten, Sugar, Dairy Free has continued to grow every week! Here are some of our testimonials:

Find our community here:
http://glutensugardairyfree.com/start-here

Testimonials

Donna: *"Thank you for all the time you have given me, the GSDF Basics, your support & creating the community support Facebook page. It has all helped this rough patch be easier. I am truly grateful for these blessings."*

Amy: *"Thank you. Thank you. THANK YOU!!! Thank you for being my guiding angel through this process. Thank you for your gracious, thoughtful, caring, kind, generous, giving, servant heart that you so obediently shared with me. Because of you my life is forever changed and I will never be the same. You are the angel God sent to me after all of this time of praying, "PLEASE, God, send me someone to help me figure this all out! I can't do this on my own! I am stronger, I am more confident, I will learn a new path, I will become a better woman and see a change in my patterns because of YOU!"*

Jean: *"Thank you again for this wonderful opportunity you gave me! I will always appreciate it.   Bless you for all you do!! Hugs!"*

Melissa: *"I am very thankful for you Michelle DeBerge and this group you created. Without all your useful information that you have given us I would have never completely cut off gluten, dairy and now sugar. I am so glad I found your class but first I found your facebook group. I have now lost 12 pounds and I feel great."*

Lila: *"Thank you Michelle for all you have done and taught us to make our Thanksgiving easier to prepare for and tips on what to look out for so we can eat healthy and not get sick."*

Donna: *"I'm grateful for Michelle DeBerge & our group. Thank you all for your support & kindness this past month. It makes all these changes much easier. XOXO"*

Jean: *"What a treat to cook when all the prep is done ahead of time! I cooked chicken fried rice, pepper steak with roasted veggies, meatballs with rice and brussel sprouts, and a beef and steamed veggie dinner. Last night was leftovers. Thank you Michelle! It's so great to get some of my independence back... And the meals are wonderful!!"*

Lisa: *"I wanted to thank you for the call yesterday. It was deeply touching to be seen, witnessed and believed in like that.. It strengthened me."*

To learn more about our events:
http://glutensugardairyfree.com/events

ACKNOWLEDGMENTS

-------**My Partner**

I would like to acknowledge my partner who saw my passion for food, flavor profiles and writing recipes. He encouraged me to write all my recipes into new gluten, sugar, dairy free ones and built me the website to showcase them. That website turned into more than a recipe site as the community grew and we became an education and information site as well.

He supported me even when I got overwhelmed, doubted my ability to get everything done and always encourages me. His brilliant ideas of how to get this information out to those that most desperately need it has been invaluable. I am blessed to have him by my side, guiding me, supporting me and always being there no matter what or the miles that sometimes separate us. Because of him, I am able to follow my passion and for that I am grateful.

-------**Dr. John DeWitt**

I would like to acknowledge my friend and collaborator Dr. John DeWitt. Dr. John DeWitt has come aboard this year as the GSDF Health and Wellness Expert. He volunteers his time on The Artichoke Series teaching health and wellness and answering nutrition questions from the audience. John is always available to explain any medical questions I have or my clients have.

His work complements what we do here at GSDF. He is a partner in one of Southern California's most revered Health and Wellness Center where people travel from all over the world for treatment. Dr. DeWitt believes in the mind, body, spirit approach to health and wellness. He has just published another book called You Don't Need Your Glasses or Contacts: Natural Ways to Correct Your Vision Without Drugs or Corrective Lenses and has a new site called Relax to Clarity http://relaxtoclarity.com/ He also has another site http://drjohndewitt.com that has a whole section about GSDF and nutrition. I am thrilled with our collaboration and the community adores Dr. John when he joins us live!

-------**Justin and Kate Stellman, Extreme Health Radio**

Justin and Kate Stellman are dear friends and we love to collaborate together. They are the founders and radio hosts of the very popular online radio show called Extreme Health Radio. They have interviewed over 300 alternative health professionals and share a wealth of information between the two of them.

Justin joins me on the GSDF Artichoke Series on a regular basis. We talk about how the balance of Mind, Body and Spirit works for optimal health. How to balance the three to achieve your health goals and discourage illness. He discusses how his personal practices have helped his health and lifestyle.

Kate joins me on the Artichoke Series to discuss women's health issues. We will be working together in the new year to open the GSDF Women's Garden where it will be a safe place for women to talk about body image, women's health issues and so much more. Long term plans include women's retreats.

You can listen to their show online and find them on FaceBook. They interview some amazing world healers. They also have a special gift for the GSDF Community. http://www.extremehealthradio.com/gsdf

-------Dr. Arinn Testa, Psy D.

Dr. Arinn Testa is a dear friend and collaborator with GSDF. She comes on board to discuss stress and the emotional brain as well as ways to manage grief, health issues and loss. Dr. Testa helps teach us what the brain does in regards to our behaviors, our illness and how to create healthy change. Dr. Testa is the founder of Holistic Psychotherapy of Marin and is the Director of Clinical Training at EBT Connect. She always takes the time to answer questions from the GSDF Community when she is live. http://www.arinntesta.com/

Thank you to my friends that have pitched in to help me get done what needed to get done to be able to publish this second book:

Carol Neu - Who constantly helps me, supports me and gives advice.

Carmen Gendraw - Who cheers me on, mails out all the books and keeps track of the customers.

Susie Back - Who's beautiful work creates my covers for all the digital books as well as the published books, who believes in me and supports me.

Monica Doherty - Who supports me and helps Susie with the work.

Jannelle Ewer - Who donates her time to help with proofreading, fixing content and who is a big support to me.

Lila Wiley - Our first GSDF Community member who always goes out of her way to help others in our community, helps test things with me and is always a huge support and ray of sunshine to me.

visit our website:
http://glutensugardairyfree.com

Introduction

GSDF is short for Gluten, Sugar and Dairy Free. Whether you have food allergy, sensitivity or other medical condition, or you are giving up gluten, sugar and/or dairy by choice, it can be quite overwhelming knowing what is safe to eat, how to cook a different way and what to have on hand to make healthy meals.

I had to become gluten, sugar, dairy free for health reasons and at first it was a struggle. As I began to study with some of the top alternative care practitioners and began to learn how and what to eat for my health, I struggled to find recipes that were all three: gluten, sugar and dairy free. Most recipes were normally just free of one of the ingredients. So I began to re-write my cookbooks so that all of my new recipes were GSDF.

I discovered the health benefits of herbs, juicing and found healthy ways to recreate some of my favorite dishes. Along the way I have lost over 200 pounds and am still getting healthy. I started a website that grew into a huge community where I teach cooking classes, educational classes about being GSDF, budget friendly classes, holiday classes and more. We have an Artichoke Series that features guest experts teaching health and wellness with live Q&A.

This book is a collection of the most popular recipes off of my website and from my digital cookbooks. Every Wednesday new recipes are featured.

All the recipes are gluten, sugar and dairy free. The average prep time for the recipes are 15 minutes or less so that they are easy to do even if you are not well. I pride myself on using normal, simple and fresh ingredients that can be found at most supermarkets. I do not use strange, expensive ingredients that you would only use once!

Michelle E. DeBerge

Contents

APPETIZERS

Cilantro Grilled Shrimp 20
Curry Sweet Potato Wedges 21
Eggplant And Parsley Dip 22
Grilled Artichoke With Lemon Aioli 23
Lemon Cauliflower 24
Spicy Honey Mustard Chicken Wings 25
Stuffed Cabbage Rolls 26
Thai Chicken Skewers 28
Thai Inspired Almond Nut Sauce 29
Veggie Spring Rolls 30
Vinegar Chile Chicken Wings 31
Warm Herb Olives 32

BEEF

Asian Inspired Ground Beef 34
Baked Beef Stroganoff 35
Beef Gyro Lettuce Wraps 36
Boneless Short Rib Ragu 37
Broccoli Beef 39
Classic Pot Roast 41
Coffee Rubbed Steak 42
Cuban Picadillo 44
Ginger Mushroom Beef 45
Greek Meatballs 46
Green chili Meatloaf 47
Herb Crusted Beef Tenderloin 49
Salisbury Steak with Mushroom Gravy 50
Sheppard's Pie 52
Slow Cooker Corn Beef – not published 53
Slow Cooker German Style Pot Roast 54

    Slow Cooker Pepper Steak 55
    Steak Diane with Mushrooms 56
    Stuffed Cabbage Rolls 58
    Swiss Steak 60

BREAKFAST
    Bacon Kale Frittata 62
    Banana Pancakes 63
    Chicken Apple Stuffed Peppers 64
    Mexican Style Eggs 65
    Overnight Banana Chocolate Oatmeal 66
    Veggie and Herb Casserole 67

GLUTEN FREE PASTA
    Acorn and Butternut Squash Lasagna 70
    Hemp Seed Pesto 72
    Lemon Asparagus Noodles 73
    Vegan Alfredo Sauce 75
    Vegan Basil Cream Sauce 76
    Zucchini Noodle Lasagna 77

PORK
    Andouille Sausage, red beans and rice 80
    Apple Cranberry Stuffed Pork Roast 81
    Apple Roasted Pork Tenderloin 83
    Ham and White Bean Soup 85
    Roasted Pork Chops 86
    Tuscan Pork 87

POULTRY
    Baked Chicken and Mushrooms 90
    Chicken Apple Stuffed Peppers 91
    Chicken Bella 92
    Chicken Cacciatore 93
    Chicken Divan Casserole 95

Chicken Fajitas 96
Chicken Kabobs 97
Chipotle Chicken 99
Classic Roast Chicken 100
Creamy Mushroom Chicken 101
Crockpot Chicken Taco Chili 102
Easy Chicken Piccata 103
Gourmet Chicken Stroganoff 105
Grilled Mustard Chicken 107
Lemon Tarragon Chicken 108
Orange Roast Chicken Breasts 109
Roast Garlic Chicken 110
Slow Cooker White Chicken Chili 111
Spicy Chicken Legs 112
Spicy Honey Mustard Chicken Wings 114
Spinach and Mushroom Stuffed Chicken Breasts 115
Thai Chicken Skewers 116
Thai Mango Chicken Curry 117
Vinegar Chile Chicken Wings 119

SALAD

Beet Orange Salad 122
Best Cobb Salad 123
Curry Chicken Salad 125
German Potato Salad 126
Green Papaya Salad 127
Grilled Caesar Salad 128
Grilled Caesar Salad 128
Grilled Chicken Asian Salad 129
Lemony Quinoa Tabouli 130
Lentil Salad 131
Seaweed Salad 133
Spicy Thai Steak Salad 134
Sugar Snap Pea Salad 135

Sweet Potato Salad with Fresh Dill 136
Tomato Avocado Salad 137

SALAD DRESSINGS

Avocado Salad Dressing 140
Caesar Dressing... 141
Garlic Lemon Sunflower Dressing 142
Honey Mustard Dressing 143
Mustard Balsamic Vinaigrette 144
Pear vinaigrette 145
Ranch Dressing 146

SEAFOOD

Cilantro Grilled Shrimp 148
Fish en Papillote.. 149
Fish Taco Bowls 151
Garlic Shrimp 152
Halibut Kebabs.. 153
Halibut with Mango Salsa 154
Lemon Rosemary Salmon 155
Pecan Dill Crusted Salmon.. 156
Red Snapper Veracruz Style 157
Shrimp with Tomatoes and Olives 158
Tequila Orange prawns.. 159

SIDE DISHES

Aloo gobi – Indian cauliflower and Potatoes........................... 162
Bacon Kale Frittata... 164
Cauliflower Fried Rice 165
Cauliflower with Lemon and Olives 166
Cilantro Spaghetti Squash 167
Coconut Rice 168
Garlic Mashed Potatoes 169

Garlic Oven Asparagus 170
Garlic Spaghetti Squash 171
Green Beans and Mushrooms 172
Herb Garlic Brown Rice 173
Herb Sweet Potato Wedges 174
Honey Glazed Carrots 175
Mushroom Risotto 176
Perfect Green Beans 177
Pesto Green Beans 178
Roasted Red Potatoes and Garlic 179
Sautéed Spinach 180
Steamed Zucchini 182
Stuffed Zucchini 183
Sweet Potato and Turnip Puree 184

SOUPS

Asparagus Herb Soup 186
Beef and Quinoa Soup 187
Carne Asada Bean Soup 188
Celery Root and Apple Soup 190
Chicken tortilla Soup 191
Easy Broccoli Soup 193
Fennel and Kale Soup with White Beans 194
Fire Roasted Tomato Soup 195
Greek Wedding Soup 196
Hearty Vegetable Soup 197
Lentil Soup 198
Potato Leek Soup 199
Pumpkin and Carrot Soup 200
Roasted Eggplant Soup 201
Spicy Parsnip Soup 202
Thai chicken Coconut Soup (Tom Kha Gai) 203

SWEET TREATS

Avocado Chocolate Mousse 206
Banana Pancakes 207
Chocolate Chia Seed Pudding 208
Cinnamon Baked Apples 209
Overnight Banana Chocolate Oatmeal 210
Pumpkin Bars 211
Quick Coconut and Chia Seed Pudding 213
Wine Poached Pears 214

VEGETARIAN

Baked Portobello Mushrooms 216
Curry Sweet Potato Wedges 217
Fall Vegetable Curry 218
Grilled Artichoke with Lemon Aioli 219
Hemp Seed Pesto 220
Layered Ratatouille 221
Lemon Cauliflower 223
Lentils and Rice (Mujadrah) 224
Moroccan Inspired Veggie Chickpea Soup 225
Quinoa Enchilada Bake 226
Quinoa Root Veggie Stuffed Cabbage 227
Shepherd's Pie 229
Spicy Indian Dal (lentils) 230
Stuffed Eggplant 232
Stuffed Poblano Pepper 233
Sweet Potato Enchiladas 235
Thai Inspired Almond Nut Sauce 236
Vegan Alfredo Sauce 237
Vegetarian Chili 238
Warm Herb Olives 239

Appetizers

Cilantro Grilled Shrimp 20
Curry Sweet Potato Wedges 21
Eggplant And Parsley Dip 22
Grilled Artichoke With Lemon Aioli 23
Lemon Cauliflower 24
Spicy Honey Mustard Chicken Wings 25
Stuffed Cabbage Rolls 26
Thai Chicken Skewers 28
Thai Inspired Almond Nut Sauce 29
Veggie Spring Rolls 30
Vinegar Chile Chicken Wings 31
Warm Herb Olives 32

CILANTRO GRILLED SHRIMP

Easy dish to make and goes great with a variety of dips. Or make a batch with saffron rice for a main meal.

SERVES 10, PREP: 10, COOK: 5 MIN

Ingredients

- ½ bunch cilantro, chopped
- 2 tablespoons olive oil
- 3 garlic cloves, minced
- 1 lime, juiced and zest
- ½ teaspoon salt
- 2 pounds uncooked medium shrimp, peeled and deveined

1. In a large resealable plastic bag, combine the cilantro, oil, lime juice, lime zest, salt and garlic. Add the shrimp; seal bag and turn to coat. Cover and refrigerate for 1 hour.
2. Thread shrimp onto skewers. Grill, covered, over medium heat for 2-3 minutes on each side or until shrimp start to turn pink and begin to shape the letter "c". Do not over cook, they will continue to cook once removed from heat.

APPETIZERS

CURRY SWEET POTATO WEDGES

Super easy to make and full of finger licking flavor. I usually cut my sweet potatoes into wedges because it is faster prep and the guests can pick up two or 3 for their snack. Much easier than making them into long fries.

SERVES 12; PREP: 15; COOK: 25 MIN

Ingredients

- 9 medium sweet potatoes, cut lengthwise into ¼" wedges
- 5 tablespoons coconut oil
- 4 teaspoons curry
- 2 teaspoons smoked paprika
- 3 teaspoons ground ginger
- 1½ teaspoons salt
- freshly ground black pepper

1. Heat oven to 425°
2. Peel the sweet potatoes and cut into wedges.
3. In a large bowl toss potato wedges with melted coconut oil, curry, paprika, ginger, salt, and pepper. Coating each piece well with the spice mixture.
4. Arrange in a single layer on a baking sheet.
5. Cook, turning once, until crisp and browned on all sides, about 20-25 minutes.

EGGPLANT AND PARSLEY DIP

This is a Greek dip and is actually called: Melintzanosalata. It is a smokey dip that originated from Kea, Greece. If I can not use my grill for this I cook the eggplants in a very high oven 450 degrees.

SERVES 10; PREP 10; COOK 30

Ingredients
- 2 large eggplants
- ½ cup extra-virgin olive oil
- 1 green bell pepper, cored and cut into pieces
- 1 jalapeño, seeded, deveined and cut into pieces
- ½ head of flat-leaf parsley leaves, chopped
- 2 tablespoons red wine vinegar
- 3 cloves garlic, minced
- ½ to 1 teaspoon salt
- fresh black pepper

1. Heat a gas grill to high. Grill eggplants, turning, until charred and soft, 18 to 20 minutes. Let cool.   Or
2. In a 450 degree oven, cook the eggplants until charred and soft, 20 -25 minutes. Let cool.
3. Peel eggplants; scoop out seeds. Chop eggplants; drain in strainer for 30 minutes.
4. Heat ¼ cup oil in a large skillet over medium-high heat.
5. Add the chopped bell pepper and cook for 10 minutes.
6. Add the jalapeño and continue cooking until soft, about 5 min.
7. Transfer to the food processor. Add the eggplant, remaining oil, parsley, vinegar, and garlic.
8. Process until slightly chunky. Season with salt and pepper.
9. Let chill before serving.

APPETIZERS

GRILLED ARTICHOKE WITH LEMON AIOLI

I love grilled artichokes with a nice dip. It is so easy to make and has a very nice wow factor when served as an appetizer.

SERVES 12; PREP: 15; COOK: 30

Ingredients
- 6 artichokes
- ½ cup good olive oil
- 3 tablespoons chopped parsley
- 1 tablespoon paprika
- 2 teaspoons salt

Easy Lemon Aioli Dip
- 2 cups good mayo
- 3 lemons, juiced and zested

1. Cook the artichokes: Steam bottom sides up until fork tender or you can easily pull a leaf out about 15-20 minutes.
2. Set aside to cool.
3. Once cool, cut the tops off of the artichokes and then cut in half lengthwise.
4. Using a spoon scrape out the thorns and thistles from the inside. May be done one day ahead. Put into fridge and chill.
5. Heat a BBQ up over medium high heat.
6. Using a pastry brush, brush olive oil over the inside and outside of the artichoke including the stem.
7. Sprinkle both sides with salt and paprika.
8. Cook over medium high heat to get a good char on both sides.
9. Put onto platter and sprinkle with chopped parsley.

Quick Lemon Aioli: Mix the juice of the lemons, the zest from the lemons into the good mayo. It will be a bit watery. Put into a container with a lid and put into fridge for 2 hours to set up.

LEMON CAULIFLOWER

This is a great tasty appetizer that is crunchy, tender and full of lemon flavor. Make a big batch and stick some toothpicks in and watch it get gobbled up. Very good room temperature so you can make this ahead.

SERVES 10; PREP: 10; COOK: 15

Ingredients

- 1 head cauliflower (about 2 pounds), cored and cut into 1" florets
- Zest of two lemons
- Juice of two lemons
- 1 teaspoon turmeric
- 1 teaspoon cayenne
- 1 teaspoon salt
- freshly ground black pepper
- 3 tablespoons coconut oil

1. Bring a large pot of salted water to a boil; add cauliflower and cook until just tender, about 5 minutes.
2. Transfer to an ice bath until chilled; drain and dry completely with kitchen towels.
3. Sprinkle the cauliflower with the lemon zest, turmeric, cayenne, salt and pepper.
4. Heat coconut oil in a skillet.
5. Cooking in batches over medium high heat, brown the cauliflower.
6. Plate and sprinkle lemon juice over.

SPICY HONEY MUSTARD CHICKEN WINGS

These wings disappeared from the plate Thursday night while watching pre-season football! They are a little messy but worth the mess! They come out spicy, tangy, sweet and delicious. Chicken wings and football is one of my favorite combinations so I like a variety of wings. This one is a sure winner.

SERVES:4; COOK: 40; PREP: 10

Ingredients
- 2 pounds chicken wings, flats and drummy seperated
- ½ cup local raw organic honey
- ⅓ cup Dijon mustard
- 2 tablespoons bourbon
- 1½ tablespoons tamari or coconut aminos
- ½ teaspoon red pepper flakes
- ¼ teaspoon salt
- 2 teaspoons sriracha (add more for more heat)
- 1½ tablespoons coconut oil

1. Pre heat oven to 400 degrees F.
2. In a medium size sauce pan, add all the ingredients and simmer while constantly stirring for 3 minutes.
3. Put the wings on a cooling rack on top of a large baking sheet. Spreading them out so that the air can circulate around them.
4. Put into oven cook 20 minutes, flip them over and another 20 minutes. they should be nice and golden.
5. You can put them under the broiler at this point for a few moments to make them a little more crispy.

STUFFED CABBAGE ROLLS

This is a classic dish that has season ground beef rolled in a cabbage leaf and then baked in a nice tomato sauce. Some versions are spicy, some are sweeter. This is a nice hearty meal with a big green salad as a side dish. When my friend had her baby, my gift to her was three weeks of all the dinners. She already had 2 small children. So I knew this would be a better gift than a new baby blanket.

I sent food over one week at a time in bulk. It had to be easy and tasty as well as kid friendly. Most were dishes they could put into the oven and serve with a salad and I also sent a few other side dishes. The stuffed cabbage is a perfect dish to make for a family. It is budget friendly, tasty and freezes well.

PREP: 15; COOK: 60 MIN; SERVES:4 EASY

Ingredients
- 1 pound ground beef
- 1 head of cabbage, green or napa
- 1 small yellow onion, diced
- 2 cloves garlic, minced
- 1 tablespoon fresh flat parsley, chopped
- 1 tablespoon tomato paste
- 1 cup cooked brown rice
- 1 egg
- 1 tablespoon coconut oil
- ½ teaspoon salt
- ¼ teaspoon black pepper

For Sauce:
- 1 tablespoon coconut oil
- 1 can of crushed tomatoes
- 2 garlic cloves, minced
- ¼ cup white wine
- ¼ cup chicken or vegetable stock
- ¼ teaspoon salt
- fresh ground black pepper

1. Make the sauce by melting the coconut oil into a saucepan and adding the garlic. Salute for one minute.
2. Add the tomatoes, wine, stock, salt and pepper. Let simmer 5 minutes.
3. In a large stock pot, fill with water and bring to a boil.
4. Take the cabbage and cut the center core out of it carefully.

5. Remove the leaves one by one keeping them whole and intact. You will need 12 leaves.
6. Add them gently to the boiling water and blanch them for 5 minutes. Pull out of pot and cool either by submerging them into a bowl of ice water and then laying them out. Or by running them under cool water and then laying them out.
7. Once the leaves are laid out on a large cutting board, cut out the center thick part of the vein, keeping the leave intact so that they will roll better.
8. In a cooking skillet over medium heat, add the coconut oil.
9. Sauté your onion and garlic in the coconut oil until soft for about 5 min, making sure to stir and not burn the garlic.
10. Add the tomato paste, parsley and ½ cup of the tomato sauce and mix. Take off the heat.
11. In a large bowl add the egg, the cooked rice, the meat and the onion mixture. Mix well.
12. Line a casserole dish with the left over cooked cabbage leaves.
13. Take about ⅓ cup of the meat mixture on one end of a cabbage leaf. toll it up while tucking in the sides. Place the cabbage roll seam side down in the casserole dish. Do this for all the leaves.
14. Pour the sauce over the rolls and bake uncovered in the oven for an hour.
15. Serve the cabbage rolls with some of the sauce spooned over the top.

THAI CHICKEN SKEWERS

These Thai Chicken Skewers have so much flavor that you can eat them as is but they are also very good dipped into the Thai Inspired Almond Nut Sauce.

SERVES: 10; PREP: 10; COOK: 5-7

Ingredients

- 2 pounds of chicken breast cut into strips (or use chicken tender pieces)
- ½ cup coconut aminos
- 4 tablespoons fresh lime juice
- 4 teaspoons fresh grated ginger
- 1 1/12 teaspoons red chili flakes
- 8-10 green onions chopped into 1 inch pieces (using the white and green parts)
- 1 teaspoon gram marsala curry powder

1. Mix all the ingredients except the chicken in a large plastic zip bag. If you want a little more marinade add a little water.
2. Once mixed, add the chicken strips and place in fridge.
3. Marinate 4 hours to overnight. This allows the flavor to go deep into the chicken.
4. BBQ: Place the strips on a well heated BBQ, turning once. Takes about 3-4 minutes per strip. Make sure you cook the chicken all the way through.
5. STOVE TOP: Heat a non-stick frying pan over medium heat and cook the strips turning once.

THAI INSPIRED ALMOND NUT SAUCE

I love a good peanut sauce with my chicken satays when I go out for Thai food. I have discovered something better, this sauce! I use this sauce on my Thai Chicken Satays that I put into butter lettuce leafs. I also use this when I make Thai Fresh Spring Rolls. It is a sauce that can drizzle nicely over the goodies in the lettuce leaves and has a bit of a bite.

PREP: 15; COOL: 0; SERVES: 3

Ingredients

- ½ cup almond nut butter
- ½ cup unsweetened coconut milk
- 1¼ teaspoon rice vinegar
- 2 tablespoons tamari
- ½ teaspoon crushed red pepper flakes
- ½ teaspoon fresh grated ginger or 1 teaspoon ground ginger
- 3 tablespoons fresh lime juice
- ¼ teaspoon cayenne pepper

1. Put all the ingredients into a blender and blend well.
2. This can be done in a food processor also.
3. If you want thiner consistency add more coconut milk.

VEGGIE SPRING ROLLS

These springs rolls are always a hit. I make them the day before, wrap each roll in a damp paper towel and put into a sealed container that I can take most of the air out. Day of the party I cut in half so the guests can see the insides. Variety of dips near by. I like the Thai Inspired Almond Nut Sauce with these.

SERVES: 12; PREP: 15

Ingredients
- 12 rice paper rounds
- ½ container dried rice noodles, cooked
- 1 red bell pepper
- 1 English cucumber
- 3 carrots
- 12 butter lettuce leaves
- bean sprouts (optional)
- 6 shrimp (sliced in half, optional)

1. Slice all the veggies into match sick size pieces except the lettuce.
2. Cook the rice noodles according to package directions and let cool.
3. Fill a large bowl with warm water.
4. Gently put one round in the water at a time holding the edges, as it starts to become pliable, remove from water and put on cutting board.
5. Starting at the edge, lay the lettuce leaf down.
6. Then lay down the veggies, some of each kind and the rice noodles.
7. Roll like a burrito pulling the ends in.
8. Once rolled wrap in a damp paper town and put into a zip bag in the fridge.
9. When ready to serve, cut in half and serve with the option of a few dips.

VINEGAR CHILE CHICKEN WINGS

These chicken wings turn out sweet, spicy and tangy. Marinade them over night for the best flavor. You can either grill them the next day or bake them in the oven. These wings are a great snack on game day! Even cold the next day they are wonderful.

SERVES 4; PREP 10; COOK: 45

Ingredients

- 2 pounds chicken wings, tips removed and flats and drumettes separated
- ½ cup rice vinegar
- 2 tablespoons coconut oil
- 7 cloves of garlic, smashed
- 1 teaspoon red chili flakes
- 1 tablespoon honey
- 1 teaspoon salt
- 2 limes
- 2 teaspoons cumin
- 1 teaspoon hot chili powder

1. In a large zip plastic bag add the chilies, vinegar, coconut oil, garlic and salt to the bag. Shake to mix well.
2. Add the chicken wings to the bag and make sure every one gets coated with the marinade. Set in fridge over night.
3. Pre heat oven to 375 f or the bbq.
4. Remove wings from bag and pat dry.
5. in a bowl add 1 tablespoon coconut oil,cumin and chili powder, mix well.
6. Toss the wings in this mix and either bbq or lay on baking racks on baking sheets.
7. If cooking on BBQ: cook 15-20 minutes turning half way through.
8. If cooking in oven: bake 40-45 minutes turning half way through.
9. Plate and then zest the zest of one lime over the wings and squeeze the juice of both limes over the wings.
10. Serve and enjoy!

WARM HERB OLIVES

I like to use a mix of pitted and not pitted olives and a mix of types in this dish. The warm olives with garlic, lemon and rosemary is always a hit.

SERVES: 12; PREP: 10; COOK: 12

Ingredients
- ½ cup extra-virgin olive oil
- zest of 2 lemons
- 2 small rosemary sprigs
- 5 garlic cloves, thickly sliced
- 6 cups of mixed oil- and brine-cured olives (Kalamata, Niçoise, Moroccan, cracked green Sicilian and Cerignola)

1. In a medium saucepan, combine the oil with the lemon zest, rosemary sprigs and garlic.
2. Cook over low heat until the garlic just begins to brown, 10-12 minutes. This will infuse the olive oil with flavor.
3. Remove from the heat, stir in the olives and let stand covered for at least 15 minutes before serving so they soak up the flavor.

Beef

Asian Inspired Ground Beef 34
Baked Beef Stroganoff 35
Beef Gyro Lettuce Wraps 36
Boneless Short Rib Ragu 37
Broccoli Beef 39
Classic Pot Roast 41
Coffee Rubbed Steak 42
Cuban Picadillo 44
Ginger Mushroom Beef 45
Greek Meatballs 46
Green chili Meatloaf 47
Herb Crusted Beef Tenderloin 49
Salisbury Steak with Mushroom Gravy 50
Sheppard's Pie 52
Slow Cooker Corn Beef – not published 53
Slow Cooker German Style Pot Roast 54
Slow Cooker Pepper Steak 55
Steak Diane with Mushrooms 56
Stuffed Cabbage Rolls 58
Swiss Steak 60

ASIAN INSPIRED GROUND BEEF

like this recipe because it is quick, easy and full of flavor. The ground beef can be served over rice or in lettuce wraps. This is one of my quick go to dinners when I am feeling like wanting take out! It takes less time to make than to order in. This dish is great served over rice or in lettuce wraps.

SERVES: 4; PREP: 5; COOK: 15

Ingredients
- 1 pound ground beef
- 3 cloves garlic, minced
- ½ yellow onion, minced
- 2 green onions, thinly sliced
- ½ cup coconut sugar
- ¼ cup tamari, coconut aminos or gluten free soy sauce
- 1 tablespoon sesame oil
- ½ teaspoon crushed red-pepper flakes
- ½ teaspoon ground ginger

1. Cooked rice or lettuce leaves for serving
2. 2 tablespoons chopped fresh cilantro
3. In a bowl, whisk together coconut sugar, tamari, sesame oil, red pepper flakes and ginger until mixed well.
4. In a large skillet add the ground beef and using a wooden spoon, begin to break up the meat.
5. Add the minced onion and garlic to the ground beef.
6. Using the wooden spoon, break up the clumps of beef as you incorporate the onions and garlic to the meat mixture.
7. Cook the meat mixture until it is no longer pink, about 8 minutes.
8. Drain off any excess fat and put meat back into the pan
9. Stir in the sauce mixture from the bowl into the ground beef mixture.
10. Cook for 3 minutes over medium heat.
11. Turn off the heat.
12. Add the sliced green onions and stir.
13. Sprinkle the chopped cilantro over the meat.
14. Serve the meat over rice or in a lettuce leaf.

BAKED BEEF STROGANOFF

I love creamy beef stroganoff and it is one of my go to comfort foods. This recipe turns out great every time and it is so easy. There is no browning of the meat, saluting of the veggies or long work in the kitchen.

You mix up all the ingredients and bake. The oven does all of the hard work for you! It turns out creamy, with a nice sauce and a beefy mushroom flavor that is brightened by the thyme and the lemon in the cashew cream.

This also makes the perfect left over dish the next day! Easy, delicious and good enough for company!

PREP: 10; COOK: 60; SERVES 4

Ingredients
- 1 lb thin sliced sirlion beef
- ½ yellow onion diced
- 2 minced garlic cloves
- 8 ounces mushrooms sliced
- 1 cup coconut milk
- ¼ cup good white wine
- ¼ cup cashew cream
- 1 cup beef or chicken stock
- 1 tea salt
- ½ tea pepper
- 1 tea thyme

1. Pre heat oven to 350
2. Slice the mushrooms, mince the garlic and dice the onion. Put all of the ingredients into a large bowl and mix well.
3. Pour into a baking dish and cover. Bake for 30 minutes. Uncover, stir, cover again and bake for another 30 minutes.
4. Serve over cooked gluten free noodles, rice or quinoa.

BEEF GYRO LETTUCE WRAPS

Greek Gyro

When I first had to become gluten, sugar, dairy free I was afraid I would never have another Greek Gyro. I loved the soft pita filled with the seasoned meat and I always put double the Tzatziki. I loved the yogurt sauce with mint and cucumber. Now I have found a way to replicate that here. I love using butter lettuce leaves as my wrap because they are so soft and pliable. The use of cashew cream makes a great sauce. Feel free to add a little garlic and vinegar to the sauce if you want it to be a little more authentic.

PREP 15; COOK 15; SERVES 4

Ingredients
- 1 pound ground beef
- ½ yellow onion, finely diced
- 2 cloves garlic finally minced
- ½ teas oregano
- 2 tbl chopped parsley
- ½ tea salt
- ¼ tea black pepper
- 1 tbl coconut oil

Sauce:
- ½ cup cashew cream
- ½ med cucumber finely diced
- 4 mint leaves finely minced
- 8 butter lettuce leaves or romaine leaves
- 1 chopped tomato
- ½ thinly sliced purple onion

1. In a large bowl combine the beef, onion, garlic, oregano, parsley, salt and black pepper. Form into 8 meat balls.

2. Heat a frying pan over medium heat and melt the coconut oil. Then add the meat balls cooking 12-15 minutes until done. OR Heat the oven to 350 degrees. Put the meat balls on a sheet tray and bake for 15-20 minutes until done.

3. In a small bow combine the ingredients for the sauce: cashew cream, cucumber and mint mixing well.

4. Arrange two lettuce leaves on top of each other on plate. Put two meat pieces in the leaf, spoon some sauce over the meat, sprinkle onion and tomato over the top.

BONELESS SHORT RIB RAGU

This short rib recipe is such an easy dish to make but packed with flavor. I find I like it best the second day so I usually Make it a day ahead. The trick with this dish is to take your time browning the meat. The darker the brown on the meat is, the deeper the flavor of the sauce. I serve this over some oven baked polenta and have been known to dish a bowl of this up with aside salad on its own.

SERVES 4-6; PREP: 15, COOK:

Ingredients

- 2 to 3 pounds beef chuck boneless short ribs
- 3 tablespoons coconut oil
- 2 slices bacon, diced
- 1 yellow onion, diced
- 2 carrots, peeled and diced
- 2 ribs celery, diced
- 5 cloves garlic
- 1 8-ounces container baby bella mushrooms, sliced thick
- 2 tablespoons tomato paste
- 1 cup good red wine
- 1 can crushed tomatoes or fire roasted dice tomatoes
- ½ salt
- fresh ground black pepper

1. Preheat oven to 325 degrees.
2. Heat a large oven proof pot over medium high heat.
3. Pat the short ribs dry and season them generously with salt and pepper.
4. Add the coconut oil to the pan, let melt and add the short ribs in one layer.
5. Let them sear uninterrupted for about five minutes. They will be able to move once don't, don't force them. There will be a lot of steam and smoke coming from the pot, this is normal.
6. Turn them over and brown the other side until they have a nice brown crust.
7. Remove the short ribs from the pan and place them on a large plate.

Continued ➜

BONELESS SHORT RIB RAGU *Continued*

8. Add the bacon and cook until it is beginning to crisp.
9. Add the onion, carrot, mushrooms, garlic and celery and a bit of salt and pepper and sauté until the vegetables are tender, scraping any brown bits from the bottom of the pan as the vegetables soften.
10. Add the tomato paste and cook, stirring, for a minute.
11. Add the tomatoes and the wine next, stirring to combine.
12. Place the short ribs into the sauce, pour in any juice from the plate into the pot.
13. Put the lid on the pot and put into the oven to cook for 2 1/12 - 3 hours. It will be fork tender when it is ready.
14. Pull the meat into shreds and chunks with a tongs and a fork and stir it into the sauce.
15. Serve over polenta or on its own.

BROCCOLI BEEF

Broccoli beef was something I always seemed to order when I had Chinese food. I loved the tender meat, crunchy broccoli and the flavorful gravy. Normally this dish is made with soy sauce, hoisin sauce or even plum sauce, all of which are not on a GSDF eating plan.

This recipe with the fresh garlic, ginger and tamari has a ton of flavor and you will never miss the other ingredients. It has great flavor and the right amount of heat with the touch of the red pepper flakes. Now you can quickly make the dish you use to order for take out in less time than it takes for delivery!

PREP: 10; COOK: 15; SERVES: 4

Ingredients
- 2 lbs thin sliced beef (bottom round works well)
- 3 cups broccoli florets
- ½ cup Tamari or gluten free soy
- ½ teaspoon red pepper flakes
- ½ cup raw honey
- 4 tablespoons toasted sesame seeds
- 2 garlic cloves minced
- 1 tablespoon minced fresh ginger
- 3 tablespoons coconut oil
- ½ cup beef stock divided
- ¼ cup corn starch

1. In a bowl mix together the tamarin, cornstarch, honey, ginger, garlic and ¼ cup beef stock.
2. Put the sliced meat in a large bowl. Pour half of the liquid mixture over the meat and toss well, coaching all the pieces. Reserve the other half of the liquid.
3. Heat a large skillet and add the coconut oil. Once hot add the broccoli florets and stir, cook for one minute. Remove and set aside.
4. In the same skillet, add the meat in single layer and let it set for about 30 seconds to 1 minute so the side can brown. Turn over and repeat. Remove to clean plate. Make sure to work in batches, not overlapping the meat and browning the meat on both sides.

Continued ➤

BROCCOLI BEEF *Continued*

5. Pour the saved liquid and the ¼ cup beef stock into the skillet. Heat on high, stirring until it begins to thicken 1-3 minutes. Add the beef and broccoli to skillet.
6. Toss to coat al the pieces. Cook for 3-5 minutes until meat is done and broccoli is tender. Sprinkle the sesame seeds over the dish and stir.

CLASSIC POT ROAST

Some of my favorite memories of the winter include the smell of a pot roast cooking slowly in the oven. The aromas of the onions, garlic, wine and beef fill the air. I wanted to create a recipe for the single dinner because pot roast is such a classic comfort meal.

PREP TIME: 10 MINUTES; COOK TIME: 2 HOURS 35 MINUTES; SERVES: 2

Ingredients
- 1 lb chuck roast
- 2-3 red potatoes quartered
- 1 small yellow onion chopped
- 3 cloves of garlic minced
- 1-cup red wine
- 1 cup beef stock
- ½-teaspoon salt
- ¼-teaspoon pepper
- ½-teaspoon dried oregano
- 1 bay leaf
- 2 tablespoons canola oil
- ½ 15 ounce can fire roasted diced tomatoes
- 3 small carrots chunked (or 2 large ones)

1. Season meat with salt and pepper on both sides. Sear both sides of the roast in canola oil in a Dutch oven until brown. Add wine, stock, garlic, tomatoes, salt, pepper, oregano, bay leaf and onion to pan. Bring to boil. Put in 350° oven. Bake covered 1 hour 45 minutes.

2. Add potatoes and carrots to pan, stir. (Add more stock if needed to cover the ingredients) Bake 45 minutes more. Taste to see if you need to add more salt or pepper.

3. Serving suggestions: Second serving freezes well. The second half of the diced tomatoes can be frozen for another time. Use good red wine in sauce because the flavor intensifies as it cooks down.

COFFEE RUBBED STEAK

The first time I had coffee rubbed steak was years ago in Las Vegas. I was a huge Chef Bobby Flay fan and he had just opened Mesa Grill in Caesars Palace. I went with my dear friend Sam Rosales who was a chef and a foodie also. We ordered an appetizer to share that was called Blue Corn Pancake. The dish came with three homemade blue corn tortillas. In the middle of each tortilla was barbecued duck with a habanero chili star anise sauce. It was amazing.

My entire was a coffee rubbed Filet Mignon with a mushroom ancho chili sauce. I choose the entree because I had not had a coffee rubbed steak before! The idea of coffee and chili being used on a grilled steak sounded delicious. It was! In fact, the coffee rubbed steak was so flavorful, it did not even need a sauce.

I was addicted at that point. I searched the internet for coffee rub recipes and tried many. In the end I came up with my own version that I love. That is this recipe.

I normally grill my steak on my grill but you can cook the coffee rubbed steak in a cast iron pan. You heat up the pan on high heat and then add the steaks. Cooking each side for 2-3 minutes and the outside gets golden brown. Then you transfer the steak to a pre heated 425 degrees F. oven on a baking sheet. Medium rare takes 8-10 minutes and a little longer for more doneness. Remove from oven and let rest 5 minutes before serving.

SERVES 4; PREP 10; COOK 15

Ingredients

- 2 Tablespoons ancho chili powder
- 2 Tablespoons fine ground espresso coffee
- 1 Tablespoon coconut oil, melted
- 1½ Teaspoons Coconut sugar (can omit but it caramelizes the outside of the steak)
- 2 Teaspoons paprika
- 2 Teaspoons dry mustard
- 2 Teaspoons salt
- 2 Teaspoons fresh ground black pepper
- 1 teaspoon oregano
- 1 Teaspoon ground coriander

1. Pre heat your grill or ready your coals.
2. In a small bowl mix all the ingredients together well.
3. Cover the steaks on both sides with the rub making sure to rub it into the meat well. Steaks should be room temperature.
4. Let the steaks stand for 10-20 minutes to allow the flavors to penetrate the meat.
5. Grill your steak for 4-5 minutes and then turn over.
6. Grill 3-5 minutes more for medium rare, 5-7 minutes for medium and 8-10 for well done.
7. Remove the steak and let sit for 5 minutes before serving.

CUBAN PICADILL

Cuban Picadillo is a traditional dish that can be made with ground pork, beef or both. It is recognizable with the chunks of olives, tomatoes, bell pepper and potatoes. I usually like to serve it over a cilantro rice with a side of black beans.

This dish is also a great filling for lettuce wraps, mixed with eggs for a hearty scramble for brunch or on its own. It is made all over Latin America and there are many variations of the dish.

SERVES: 4; PREP: 15; COOK: 20

Ingredients

- 1½ pounds lean ground beef
- 1 green pepper, chopped
- 1 yellow onion, diced
- 1 cups tomato sauce
- ½ cup sliced pimiento-stuffed olives
- ⅓ cup raisins
- 2 tablespoons cider vinegar
- 4 medium cloves garlic, finely chopped
- 2 teaspoons ground cumin
- 2 teaspoons dried oregano
- 1 teaspoon salt
- ½ teaspoon freshly ground black pepper
- 2 bay leaves
- ½ cup dry white wine
- 1 cup diced canned tomatoes
- 1 large waxy potato (such as Yukon Gold), peeled and cut into ¼-inch cubes

1. In a large nonstick skillet, cook the beef, pepper and onion over medium heat until meat is no longer pink; drain. About 8-10 minutes.
2. Stir in the tomato sauce, garlic, cumin, oregano, teaspoons salt, pepper, vinegar and bay leaves and cook until fragrant. 2-3 minutes.
3. Add the white wine and reduce for about 5 minutes.
4. Add the olives, raisins and potatoes.
5. Cover and cook for 12 minutes or until potatoes are done.
6. Discard bay leaves.
7. Serve with rice and beans.

GINGER MUSHROOM BEEF

The Ginger Beef recipe was created one evening when I was not sure what I wanted to make for dinner, but I knew I was hungry for something with a lot of flavor and I had a piece of chateaubriand beef on hand. (Note: A nice piece of sirloin or the ready packages of sliced beef you find in the grocery store works very well in this recipe also.) My two go to beef recipes are pepper steak or beef stroganoff and I did not want either one.

SERVES: 4; PREP: 10; COOK: 15

Ingredients
- 2 minced garlic cloves
- 1 tbl coconut oil
- 1 cup baby bella mushrooms halved
- 1 cup shiitake mushrooms stems removed and halved
- 3 cups baby kale or chopped kale

Marinade:
- 1/3 cup tamari or soy
- 3/4 cup stock beef or chicken
- 3 tbs rice wine vinegar
- 3 tbs corn starch
- 1/3 tea black pepper
- 2 green onions cut into one inch pieces
- 2 tsp ground ginger

1. heat oil in pan
2. add mushrooms and garlic and cook 3 minutes.
3. add reserved marinade and cook 3-4 more minutes
4. add kale and cook until wilted
5. add reserved beef and heat through
6. sauce will thicken upon cooking.
7. Serve over rice or quinoa.

Marinade
1. thinly slice 1 pound of sirloin or chateaubriand steak
2. add steak to marinade and marinade 4-8 hours
3. heat 1 tbl coconut oil in pan
4. remove meat from marinade reserving marinade for later
5. cook over med high heat quickly until almost cooked through
6. remove to plate and set aside

GREEK MEATBALLS

A blend of ground beef and ground lamb lay the foundation for these tasty bites. Then they are packed with fresh oregano, mint and green onion. These would go well in a lettuce wrap with some sliced bell peppers and chopped mint.

SERVES 8

Ingredients

- 1 pound ground beef
- 1 pound ground lamb
- 1 yellow onion, grated
- 3 cloves garlic, minced
- ½ cup gf breadcrumbs
- 1 egg, beaten
- 2 tablespoons chopped oregano leaves
- 2 tablespoons chopped mint leaves
- 2 green onions, green part cut very thin
- 1 tablespoon cumin
- 1 teaspoon cinnamon
- zest of one lemon
- 1 teaspoon salt
- black pepper
- 1 tablespoon coconut oil

1. Pre heat oven to 450 degrees F.
2. In a skillet sauté onion and garlic until translucent, 3 minutes over medium heat.
3. In a large bowl add the beef, lamb, egg, onion, garlic, oregano, mint, breadcrumbs, green onion, cumin, cinnamon, lemon zest, salt and pepper. Using your fingers mix well but do not over mix.
4. Form mini meat balls with your hands, you should get 16 meatballs.
5. Put the meatballs on a sheet tray and place in the oven.
6. Roast until nice and brown, 15-18 minutes.

GREEN CHILI MEATLOAF

This is in no way your ordinary meatloaf. In fact it is so extraordinary that I served it as a main dish a few years ago to my annual holiday party dinner where my guests arrive in ball gowns! Yes, it is indeed that good.

Let me tell you the reason why. It is moist and spicy without too much spice. It is unique in flavor and it is packed full of flavor!

SERVES 6; PREP 10; COOK 60 MINUTES

Ingredients

- 2 Lbs. of Ground Beef
- 1 Can Fire Roasted Green Chilies
- 1 Large Carrot, peeled and minced
- 1 Yellow onion, minced
- 4 cloves garlic, minced
- 1 tablespoon. Cumin
- 1 tablespoon Red Chili Powder
- 1 teaspoon Salt
- Fresh Black Pepper
- ½ bunch Cilantro, leaves minced
- 1 egg, beaten
- Gluten Free Breadcrumbs
- 1 Tbsp. Coconut Oil
- Organic Ketchup
- ¼ teaspoon cayenne chili

1. Pre heat oven to 350 degrees F.
2. Heat a small frying pan and add coconut oil to it over medium heat. Once the oil melts, add carrot, garlic and onion. Sauté until onion becomes translucent. Set aside to cool
3. In a large bowl, beat the egg and then add the chopped cilantro to it.
4. Add the can of chilies, cumin, chili powder, salt and pepper to the egg mix and beat together.
5. To the bowl, add the beef and cooled vegetables and toss together, gently incorporating all ingredients. Don't over work the meat.
6. Start sprinkling in the breadcrumbs starting with ¼ cup and adding more, 1 Tbsp. at a time until it holds together.

Continued ➤

GREEN CHILI MEATLOAF *Continued*

7. Place in a meatloaf or an ovenproof baking dish
8. Cover the meatloaf with ketchup
9. Sprinkle the top of the ketchup with cayenne chili and bake for 1 hour at 350 degrees
10. Remove from oven and let cool for 5 minutes before slicing.

HERB CRUSTED BEEF TENDERLOIN

This meat comes out perfectly medium rare and tender every time. I love the crust of al of the fresh herbs, garlic and salt on the outside.

PREP 10; COOK 30; 6 SERVINGS

Ingredients

- 2 pounds center cut beef tenderloin, trimmed
- ¼ cup olive oil (I use garlic infused olive oil)
- 2 teaspoons chopped fresh rosemary
- 2 teaspoons chopped fresh Italian parsley
- 2 teaspoons chopped fresh thyme leaves
- 2 teaspoons chopped fresh oregano
- 2 teaspoons minced garlic
- 1 tablespoon salt
- 1 tablespoon freshly ground black pepper

1. Preheat the oven to 400 degrees F.
2. Tie the beef with butcher's string and rub with the olive oil.
3. Season the beef with salt and pepper.
4. Combine the rosemary, parsley, thyme, and garlic and pat the mixture on the beef.
5. Over high heat sear the beef in an ovenproof skillet, turning to brown on all sides, about 3 minutes each side.
6. Place the skillet directly into the oven and roast the beef for 20 to 25 minutes.
7. Let the beef rest for 10 minutes before removing the string and slicing.

SALISBURY STEAK WITH MUSHROOM GRAVY

This is my healthier version of a classic dish. It reminds me of those special occasions when as a child I was allowed to have a T.V. dinner which was a very rare occurrence. It was a special treat to eat and watch TV on trays. Salisbury steak seemed so glamorous back then. This is my grown up version that is healthier and has more flavor.

PREP TIME: 10 MINUTES; COOK TIME: 25 MINUTES; SERVING: 4

Ingredients
- 1 lb ground beef
- ½ onion minced
- 1 yellow onion sliced thin
- 4 garlic cloves minced
- 2 teaspoons steak seasoning
- 3 tablespoons gluten free breadcrumbs
- 1 tablespoon corn starch
- 3 tablespoons coconut oil divided
- 1 teaspoon salt
- ½ teaspoon fresh ground pepper
- 4 sprigs fresh thyme or ⅛ teaspoon dried
- 8 ounces baby Bella or crimini mushrooms sliced
- 1 cup beef stock

1. In a large frying pan, heat the 1 tablespoon of the coconut oil up. Add the garlic and minced onions.
2. Sauté minced onion and garlic until translucent. (Do not brown the garlic.). Put the mixture in a bowl.
3. Add to the onion mixture the ground beef, steak seasoning and breadcrumbs.
4. Make 4 oval patties with this mixture making sure that the center of the patty is slightly thinner than the outside for even cooking.
5. In the frying pan, over medium heat, melt 1 tablespoon coconut oil. Brown both sides of the patty in 1 tablespoon of coconut oil. They will not be fully cooked at this point. Put on plate, cover.

6. In the same frying pan melt 1 tablespoon of coconut oil over medium high heat. Add the sliced onions, mushrooms and thyme. Sauté the mixture but do not brown. Sprinkle with corn starch, stir and cook 2 minutes. Add beef stock, salt and pepper. Mix well.
7. Once the stock mixture is up to boil, lower heat and nestle the beef patties into the same to cook. Cook 15 minutes over medium low heat, turning once.
8. Serve the patties with the mushroom gravy over the top.

SHEPHERD'S PIE

This Shepherds Pie comes from humble beginnings but it is still a favorite comfort food. With the addition of the right seasonings we can take it to another level. This recipe uses mashed cauliflower for the topping. Feel free to substitute mashed butternut squash, mashed acorn squash or mashed sweet potato.

SERVES 6-8; PREP 15; COOK 45

Ingredients
- 1 Tbs coconut oil
- 4-6 cloves garlic, chopped
- 3 lb. ground beef
- 2 cups onions, chopped
- 2 cups carrots, chopped
- 2 stalks celery, chopped
- 1 tablespoon fresh rosemary, chopped
- 3 teaspoons fresh thyme, chopped
- 6 oz tomato paste
- 2 Tbs balsamic vinegar
- 6 c mashed cauliflower

1. Preheat the oven to 350.
2. Heat large frying pan over medium heat. Once hot, add ground beef, cooking until browned.
3. While browning mince garlic and dice onion, carrots and celery.
4. Drain the juices from ground beef and set aside.
5. Set pan on medium heat again and add oil. Once oil is hot, add onions, garlic, carrots and celery to pan on medium heat. Sauté until onion is translucent and carrot and celery are tender. Add rosemary and thyme.
6. Add browned ground beef back into pan and combine with balsamic, tomato paste and mix well.
7. Pour into baking dish and cover with mashed cauliflower.
8. Bake for 45 minutes until cauliflower begins to have areas of light golden brown.
9. Note: This may be made a day a head, covered and put into the fridge. If putting in oven from fridge cook for 60-70 minutes.

SLOW COOKER CORN BEEF

I love corn beef and found that it comes out best in the slow cooker. When making this recipe, always put the veggies underneath the meat.

SERVES 6-8; PREP: 5; COOK 8-9 HOURS

Ingredients

- 8 medium red potatoes, quartered
- 3 medium carrots, peeled and sliced
- 1 yellow onion, sliced
- 5 cloves garlic
- 1 corned beef brisket with spice packet (3 pounds)
- 1-½ cups water
- 1 orange, zest and juice
- 2 tablespoons Dijon mustard

1. Place the potatoes, carrots, garlic and onion in a 5-qt. slow cooker.
2. Cut brisket in half; place over vegetables.
3. Mix the water, orange zest, orange juice, dijon mustard and contents of spice packet together well and pour over the meat.
4. Cover and cook on low for 8-9 hours or until meat and vegetables are tender.
5. Using a slotted spoon, transfer corned beef and vegetables serving tray.

SLOW COOKER GERMAN STYLE POT ROAST

This German style pot roast has red wine, dill pickles and mustard. I love to eat it on its own or over a serving of mashed parsnips and turnips.

SERVES 6-8; PREP: 5; COOKS: 8-9 HOURS

Ingredients

- 2 ½ - 3 - pound boneless beef chuck pot roast
- 1 tablespoon coconut oil
- 2 cups carrots, cut into one inch pices
- 2 yellow onions chopped
- ¾ cup chopped GF pickles
- ½ cup red wine or beef broth
- ⅓ cup German-style mustard
- ½ teaspoon coarse ground black pepper
- ¼ teaspoon ground cloves
- 2 bay leaves

1. In the slow cooker, combine the carrot, onion, celery and pickles.
2. In a large skillet, melt the coconut oil. Add the meat and brown the meat on all sides, then place on top of the veggies.
3. In a small bowl combine the ½ cup red wine, the mustard, pepper, cloves and bay leaves. Pour over meat and vegetables in slow cooker.
4. Cover and cook on low-heat setting for 8 to 10 hours.
5. Using a slotted spoon, remove the meat and vegetables from the cooker and place on a serving platter; cover with foil to keep warm.
6. Skim the fat from the cooking liquid and take out the bay leaves.
7. Cut the meat into chunks and pour the sauce over.
8. **For a thicker gravy.** Add 1 tablespoon corn starch to 3 tablespoons of the gravy. Add to the gravy in a skillet and bring to high heat to thicken.

SLOW COOKER PEPPER STEAK

This Slow Cooker Pepper Steak is one of our most popular recipes. We get tons of comments on it. It is simple but comes out great every time. I have even served it to company and they raved. Put this one in your list of quick, easy and tasty go to recipes.

SERVES 4-6; PREP 10; COOK 4-8 HRS

Ingredients

- 2 lb sirloin, cut into strips
- 2-3 cloves garlic, minced
- 2 bell peppers, seeded and sliced
- 1 can stewed tomatoes
- ½ cup beef stock
- 1 tablespoon corn starch
- 2 tablespoons fresh grated ginger
- ½ teaspoon salt
- ½ teaspoon pepper
- 1 tablespoon chopped cilantro
- 2 or 3 lime slices

1. Heat a large frying pan on medium high heat. Once pan is hot set sirloin strips in and let sit 2-4 minutes or until they release from pan easily. Flip and brown other sides.vRemove sirloin from heat.
2. Whisk stock with cornstarch and add to slow cooker.
3. Add all the other ingredients to slow cooker and stir to combine.
4. Set slow cooker on high and cook for 3-4 hours or low for 6-8 hours.
5. Garnish with chopped cilantro and limes.

STEAK DIANE WITH MUSHROOMS

Traditionally Steak Diane is a steak that is pan fried and the sauce is made from the pan juices and some times flambeed. This is my version but with a creamy mushroom sauce. The steaks cook up nice and tender and the mushroom sauce is full of flavor. I use red wine in this recipe. Another version I like is to use ¼ cup of good cognac instead of the wine. Both versions are delicious. This is an easy dish to prepare but it has a great wow factor. Perfect for those special dinners.

Ingredients

- 6 small beef tenderloin steaks
- ½ ounce dried porcini mushrooms
- 2 cups boiling water $
- 1½ teaspoons coconut oil
- 1 tablespoon coconut oil
- ⅓ cup thinly sliced shallots
- 2 cups sliced fresh cremini mushrooms
- 3 garlic cloves, minced
- 1½ teaspoon salt, divided
- ½ teaspoon fresh black pepper
- ¼ teaspoon black pepper
- ½ cup red wine
- 2 tablespoons cashew cream or 1 tablespoon corn starch
- 2 tablespoons chopped fresh sage
- 1 tablespoon chopped fresh thyme

1. Salt and pepper both sides of all 6 filets and let stand at room temperature while you make the sauce.
2. Place porcini mushrooms in a bowl, and cover with 2 cups boiling water.
3. Let the mushrooms and water soak for 15 minutes.
4. Drain through a sieve over a bowl, reserving mushrooms and soaking liquid. Remove the mushrooms and chop into small bits keeping the soaking liquid in the bowl.
5. Heat a large saucepan over medium-high heat.
6. Add 1½ teaspoons coconut oil to pan, let melt and coat bottom of the pan.

7. Add shallots to pan, sauté for about 1 minute, stirring frequently taking care not to burn.
8. Add cremini mushrooms to pan; sauté for 2 - 3 minutes or until tender.
9. Add garlic to pan and sauté for 1 minute taking care not to burn.
10. Stir in the porcini mushrooms, salt and black pepper. Sauté 1 minute, stirring frequently.
11. Add the red wine to pan and bring to a boil.
12. Cook for 3-4 minutes or until liquid almost evaporates. This condenses the flavor.
13. If you are using corn starch, sprinkle it over mushroom mixture; cook for 1 minute, stirring frequently. Then gradually add the reserved mushroom soaking liquid, stirring constantly with a whisk and bring to a simmer.
14. If you are using the cashew cream, add the reserved mushroom soaking liquid, bring to a simmer and then whisk in the cashew cream.
15. Cook the sauce for 2 minutes or until slightly thick, stirring frequently.
16. Stir in herbs gently. Turn off heat.
17. Heat a large skillet over medium-high heat and add 1 tablespoon coconut oil.
18. Add beef to pan and sauté 4 minutes on each side or until desired degree of doneness.
19. Remove from pan; let the meat rest for 10 minutes.
20. Heat up the sauce and serve over the steaks.

STUFFED CABBAGE ROLLS

This is a classic dish that has season ground beef rolled in a cabbage leaf and then baked in a nice tomato sauce. Some versions are spicy, some are sweeter. This is a nice hearty meal with a big green salad as a side dish. When my friend had her baby, my gift to her was three weeks of all the dinners. She already had 2 small children. So I knew this would be a better gift than a new baby blanket.

I sent food over one week at a time in bulk. It had to be easy and tasty as well as kid friendly. Most were dishes they could put into the oven and serve with a salad and I also sent a few other side dishes. The stuffed cabbage is a perfect dish to make for a family. It is budget friendly, tasty and freezes well.

PREP: 15; COOK: 60 MIN; SERVES:4; EASY

Ingredients
- 1 pound ground beef
- 1 head of cabbage, green or napa
- 1 small yellow onion, diced
- 2 cloves garlic, minced
- 1 tablespoon fresh flat parsley, chopped
- 1 tablespoon tomato paste
- 1 cup cooked brown rice
- 1 egg
- 1 tablespoon coconut oil
- ½ teaspoon salt
- ¼ teaspoon black pepper

For Sauce:
- 1 tablespoon coconut oil
- 1 can of crushed tomatoes
- 2 garlic cloves, minced
- ¼ cup white wine
- ¼ cup chicken or vegetable stock
- ¼ teaspoon salt
- fresh ground black pepper

1. Make the sauce by melting the coconut oil into a saucepan and adding the garlic. Salute for one minute.
2. Add the tomatoes, wine, stock, salt and pepper. Let simmer 5 minutes.
3. In a large stock pot, fill with water and bring to a boil.
4. Take the cabbage and cut the center core out of it carefully.

5. Remove the leaves one by one keeping them whole and intact. You will need 12 leaves.
6. Add them gently to the boiling water and blanch them for 5 minutes. Pull out of pot and cool either by submerging them into a bowl of ice water and then laying them out. Or by running them under cool water and then laying them out.
7. Once the leaves are laid out on a large cutting board, cut out the center thick part of the vein, keeping the leave intact so that they will roll better.
8. In a cooking skillet over medium heat, add the coconut oil.
9. Sauté your onion and garlic in the coconut oil until soft for about 5 min, making sure to stir and not burn the garlic.
10. Add the tomato paste, parsley and ½ cup of the tomato sauce and mix. Take off the heat.
11. In a large bowl add the egg, the cooked rice, the meat and the onion mixture. Mix well.
12. Line a casserole dish with the left over cooked cabbage leaves.
13. Take about ⅓ cup of the meat mixture on one end of a cabbage leaf. toll it up while tucking in the sides. Place the cabbage roll seam side down in the casserole dish. Do this for all the leaves.
14. Pour the sauce over the rolls and bake uncovered in the oven for an hour.
15. Serve the cabbage rolls with some of the sauce spooned over the top.

SWISS STEAK

This is one of my favorite, go to easy meals to make. It not only is super easy to do but the slow cooking time fills the house with mouth watering aromas! The trick is to really sear the beef and get a good color on it. This adds a lot of flavor. When it is done cooking the meat falls apart into the lovely grave made up of the shredded veggies. So good! I grew up having this served over mashed potatoes but it is quite fine on its own.

SERVES 4-6; PREP 15; COOK 180 MINUTES

Ingredients

- 2 lbs top round steak, thinly sliced
- 4 carrots, peeled
- 1 yellow onion,
- 5 cloves garlic
- 1 large red bell pepper
- 3 stalks celery
- 8 oz tomato sauce
- ½ cup red wine
- ½ cup beef stock
- 2 tablespoons coconut oil
- ½ teaspoon salt
- ¼ teaspoon pepper

1. Pre heat the oven to 325
2. In a food processor with a shred disk, shred the carrots, onion, garlic, celery and bell pepper.
3. In a large dutch oven, heat the coconut oil. Sprinkle salt and pepper over both sides of the beef. (Do this to all the pieces.) Sear the beef on both sides until it turns a dark brown color and then put on a plate to rest.
4. Once all the meat is seared, add the veggies to the pan and sauté for 3 minutes. Remove the veggies to a bowl and add the tomato sauce, red wine and stock. Stir well.
5. Put ⅓ of the veggie mix on the bottom of the dutch oven. Add a layer of meat and then veggies. Repeat and end with veggies on top.
6. Cover and cook for 2½ -3 hours or until meat falls apart easily.
7. Cut meat up in the sauce into bit size pieces.
8. Serve over mashed potatoes, rice or gluten free pasta.

Breakfast

Bacon Kale Frittata.. 62
Banana Pancakes 63
Chicken Apple Stuffed Peppers 64
Mexican Style Eggs 65
Overnight Banana Chocolate Oatmeal 66
Veggie and Herb Casserole 67

BACON KALE FRITTATA

Frittatas are very easy to make and make a great breakfast, easy snack or even a light dinner. You can put most anything into a frittata. In this one I put bacon and kale which make a delicious combination.

SERVES 4; PREP 5; COOK 30

Ingredients

- 1 tablespoon coconut oil
- ½ yellow onion, chopped
- 4 slices bacon, chopped
- 2 cups kale, de-stemmed and chopped
- 8 large eggs
- ½ cup coconut milk (almond milk)
- ½ teaspoon salt
- black pepper

1. Pre heat oven to 350 degrees F.
2. In a large bowl beat the eggs well, add the coconut milk, salt and pepper and beat again.
3. In an oven proof skillet, heat the coconut oil over medium heat.
4. Add the bacon pieces to the pan and cook for 4 minutes.
5. Add the onion and cook 2 more minutes.
6. Add the kale to the pan and cook for 5 minutes.
7. Add the eggs to the pan, do not stir. Cook for 4 minutes over medium heat as the bottom and edges begin to set up.
8. Put the skillet in the oven and let cook 12-15 minutes or until the fritter is cooked all the way through.
9. Let it set on the counter 3-5 minutes before cutting.
10. This tastes good at room temperature also.

BANANA PANCAKES

These banana pancakes are super easy and delicious.

SERVES 2; PREP 5; COOK 5

Ingredients
- 1 Large Banana
- 2 eggs
- 1 Tsp coconut oil
- ¼ Tsp vanilla extract
- ¼ Tsp salt

1. Peel the banana and put it into a large bowl.
2. Mash the banana really well with a potato masher or fork until it is really smooth.
3. In a second bowl beat the eggs well. Add the eggs to the banana mixture along with the vanilla and salt. Mix well.
4. Or Put the peeled banana, eggs, vanilla and salt in blender and blend well.
5. In a small skillet heat the coconut oil.
6. Once the oil is heated add half of the batter. Cook like you would a normal pancake, flipping it half way through.

CHICKEN APPLE STUFFED PEPPERS

Stuffed Peppers have become a favorite breakfast for me because they are easy to assemble and the oven does the work. A great way to get protein and veggies in me first thing in the morning.

SERVES 4; PREP 5; COOK 35

Ingredients
- 4 bell peppers, cut in half, seeded and deveined
- 8 eggs, beaten
- 1 package of chicken and apple sausage, diced
- 2 cups of spinach, chopped
- ½ cup salsa
- ½ teaspoon salt
- black pepper

1. Heat oven to 350 degrees F.
2. In a large bowl mix the chopped spinach and sausage together. Put ¼ of the mix into each half of bell pepper.
3. Put the salsa in the baking dish and put peppers stuffed side up, into the baking dish.
4. In a large bowl add the eggs, salt and peer and beat well.
5. Pour egg mixture into each bell pepper.
6. Bake in oven 25-35 minutes until set and done.

MEXICAN STYLE EGGS

Since I switched to a healthy lifestyle, I take breakfast seriously these days. I use to skip breakfast or eat something unhealthy for me. I have found that I have a lot more energy when I have protein in the morning To keep it interesting and not get bored with my food, I make them a lot of different ways. The fun thing is that you can put almost any kind of veggies in them. You can also mix up your seasonings for the eggs. One way I like my eggs are scrambled Mexican style.

SERVES 1; PREP 5; COOK 3-5

Ingredients
- 2 organic eggs
- ¼ of an onion diced
- 1 small Roma tomato seeded
- 1 Serrano chili or ½ jalapeño chili
- salt and pepper to taste
- 1 teaspoon coconut oil

1. Dice the onion.
2. Seed and dice the tomato.
3. Chop the chili, removing seeds if you would like for less spice.
4. Beat the eggs in a bowl.
5. Heat a small frying pan on the stove with the coconut oil over medium low heat. Eggs taste better and have better texture if cooked over low heat.
6. Once the oil is hot add the veggies and sauté for about a minute or so, until the onion is partially cooked.
7. Add the beaten eggs and cook until desired doneness.

OVERNIGHT BANANA CHOCOLATE OATMEAL

Lets admit that sometimes we don't have time to make breakfast but we really want something divine and healthy to eat. This is a great recipe to do. You put it together, put it in the fridge overnight and in the morning you have a scrumptious feast!

PREP: 10 MIN; COOK: NONE; SERVES: 1

Ingredients

- 1 ripe banana, chopped
- 1 tablespoon raw cacao poder
- 1 cup unsweetened vanilla almond milk
- ¾ gluten free organic oats
- 1 tablespoon chia seeds
- ½ tablespoon maple syrup
- 1 tablespoon almonds or pecans, optional for topping

1. In a small mason jar, mix all ingredients except the banana until well combined.
2. Cover with a lid and refrigerate overnight (about 8 hours).
3. In the morning, mix in one chopped banana and sprinkle with nuts.

VEGGIE HERB AND EGG CASSEROLE

I have been so busy in the mornings that I wanted a quick and healthy breakfast full of protein and veggies. This recipe is delicious and you can adapt it to whatever kind of veggies you have on hand. I made a big casserole and it keeps well in the fridge and can be frozen. Healthy "fast" food! The best part of this is that it is so easy and quick to make!

Ingredients
- 12 eggs
- 1 red bell pepper diced
- 1 yellow onion diced
- 2 cups of mushrooms sliced
- 2 tablespoons cilantro chopped
- ½ teaspoon salt
- ¼ teaspoon fresh black pepper
- 1 tablespoons 1 teaspoon coconut oil divided

1. Preheat oven to 350°
2. Beat the eggs in a bowl and add the chopped cilantro, set aside.
3. Heat 1 tablespoon of coconut oil in a frying pan. Sauté the diced bell pepper, diced onion and sliced mushrooms until tender. Add the salt and pepper. About 5 minutes. Turn off heat and let the mix cool to room temperature.
4. Oil the inside of a casserole dish with 1 teaspoon of coconut oil.
5. Put the cooled veggie mix on the bottom of the dish and pour the herb and egg mixture over. Mix gently.
6. Bake in the oven for 35 minutes. The edges will brown up. Let the casserole sit on the counter for 5-10 minutes before cutting.

Notes: You can substitute any veggies or herbs you have on hand and like. The veggies in the recipe where what I had on hand that day. Add chicken sausage for another variation.

It reheats well, is great at room temperature and you can cut into individual pieces, wrap with plastic wrap, drop it into a zip freezer bag and freeze. Now you have a fast and healthy meal on hand.

Have it for dinner with a side salad or for brunch.

Gluten Free Pasta

Acorn and Butternut Squash Lasagna 70
Hemp Seed Pesto 72
Lemon Asparagus Noodles 73
Vegan Alfredo Sauce 75
Vegan Basil Cream Sauce 76
Zucchini Noodle Lasagna 77

ACORN AND BUTTERNUT SQUASH LASAGNE

This lasagne blew my dinner guests away. They did not realize that there was no cheese or dairy anywhere in it until I told them after dinner. The creaminess and mouth feel of the different squash between the layers of the gluten free noodles is divine. A nice mix of sautéed mushrooms and spinach in the middle layer adds depth to this dish. It is so easy to make and most folks will think you slaved over it.

SERVES 4-6; COOK: 2HOURS; PREP: 15 MINUTES

Ingredients

- 1 small butternut squash
- 1 small acorn squash
- 8 ounces of sliced mushrooms
- 4 cups of fresh spinach or 1 packed frozen spinach thawed
- 2 cups of marinara sauce
- ½ cup water
- 2 tablespoons coconut oil, divided
- 1 package of fresh gluten free lasagne noodles

1. Pre heat the oven to 400 degrees f.
2. Cut each squash in half and scoop out the seeds. Rub one tablespoon of coconut oil over the cut sides of the squash and sprinkle with pepper and salt.
3. Place face down on a baking sheet and bake for 1 hour. Pull out and let cool.
4. Once cooled use a fork to get all the meat out of each squash and put in separate bowls. Mash well with a fork and season with a pinch of salt and a touch of fresh black pepper.
5. Turn oven down to 325 degrees f.
6. In a large skillet melt one tablespoon of the coconut oil and sauté the mushrooms until cooked and nice and brown. Season with a pinch of salt and pepper.
7. Put in a bowl and set aside.
8. In a large skillet cook the spinach and squeeze out the excess water.

9. Place ½ cup marinara sauce and ½ cup of water in bottom of baking dish. Use a fork and mix well.
10. Put down the down the noodles over the sauce.
11. Take the mashed acorn squash and cover the bottom layer of noodles. Add ½ cup of the marinara sauce.
12. Add another layer of noodles. evenly spread the spinach and mushrooms over those noodles. sprinkle evenly over the mix ½ cup more of the marinara sauce.
13. Add the last layer of noodles. Cover with the butternut squash mash evenly. Pour the rest of the marinara sauce over the top of the lasagne.
14. Cover tightly with foil and bake for an hour.
15. Let set 10 minutes and then cut and serve.

HEMP SEED PESTO

I wanting to create a new pesto recipe and having learned about how much protein and nutrients are in hemp seeds, I thought I would experiment with using hemp seeds in pesto. After a few tries I found the perfect combination of ingredients and did not even miss the parmesan cheese like I thought I would. This easy pesto lasts up to a week in the fridge in a sealed jar.

SERVES 4-6; PREP 10; COOKS

Ingredients
- 1 cup Basil leaves, washed and spun dry
- ¼ cup Extra Virgin Olive Oil
- 1 clove garlic minced
- ½ cup Hulled Hemp Seed

1. Combine basil, garlic, and olive oil in a blender or food processor and blend to preferred texture
2. Add hemp seed and blend just until mixed.
3. Serve immediately or store in a covered container for up to a week.

LEMON ASPARAGUS NOODLES

I bought some beautiful asparagus and peas at the farmers market. It was a warm summer's night and I wanted something fresh for dinner. So I made a quinoa pasta with the veggies, garlic, and lemon. White wine, basil and mint. It was delicious! I ate the leftovers cold the next morning and it was still good!

Ingredients
- 1 tablespoon coconut oil
- 2 cups of asparagus cut into one inch pieces
- ½ cup shelled peas
- 3-4 cloves of garlic minced
- ¼ yellow onion finely minced
- 1 cup good white wine
- 1 cup chicken stock (vegetable stock works too)
- zest of a whole lemon
- juice of a whole lemon
- ¼ cup mint leaves
- ¼ cup basil leaves
- ½ teaspoon salt
- ½ teaspoon black pepper
- ½ pound any style GF noodles

1. Put a large pot of water on the stove to boil to cook the noodles. In another pot, boil some water. Add the peas and asparagus to the boiling water. Cook for two minutes. Drain and put into a bowl that has ice and water in it to shock the veggies and stop them from cooking. Drain.

2. Dice the onion very fine. Mince the garlic. I used 4 giant cloves because I wanted it to have a lot of garlic. I do all the prep ahead of time. That way cooking the meal is easier and neater!
Heat a large skillet and add the coconut oil. Once it is hot, add the garlic and onions. Cook until the onions are translucent and do not let the garlic brown. Add the white wine and let it reduce over medium heat 3-4 minutes.

3. Add the chicken stock, lemon zest, juice of the lemon, salt and pepper to the pan and reduce about 5 minutes. Taste for seasoning.

4. Cook the pasta, drain it and immediately add to the sauce. Add ¼ cup of the water from the pasta to the sauce. Toss the noodles well. Add the veggies and the herbs and toss well. Let pasta sit in pan for about 3 minutes covered so that the pasta absorbs the sauce and flavor.

VEGAN ALFREDO SAUCE

Giving up dairy does not have to mean giving up Alfredo sauce. Now and then I get a craving for a good Alfredo sauce and this is the recipe I turn to now that I am dairy free. In fact, your dinner guests might actually be shocked to learn that there is no dairy in this sauce. I added a touch of garlic to the sauce, feel free to add a few more cloves if you really want the garlic flavor.

I have found this sauce to work well over zucchini noodles, spaghetti noodles and gluten free noodles. Roast chicken or sautéed prawns are tasty in this sauce also.

PREP: 10; COOK: 10; SERVES: 4

Ingredients
- ½ cup raw whole cashews, soak for 4 hours in water
- 1 cup vegetable stock
- 1 yellow onion, finely chopped
- ½ teaspoon salt
- ½ teaspoon ground black pepper
- 2 large garlic cloves, minced
- 1 tablespoon lemon juice
- ¼ cup nutritional yeast
- 1 tablespoon coconut oil

1. In a medium skillet, heat the coconut oil over medium heat.
2. Add the finely minced onion and sauté over medium low heat. Once the onions become translucent, about 5 minutes, add the finely minced garlic. Continue to cook for 3 minutes, stirring so that nothing burns.
3. In a high speed blender add the cooked onion and garlic.
4. Drain and rinse the cashew after they soak.
5. Add the cashews, stock, lemon juice, nutritional yeast, salt and pepper to the onion/garlic mixture.
6. Blend on high until smooth and creamy.
7. Pour sauce in a medium skillet and heat up. Then serve over your desired noodles: zucchini noodles, rice noodles or gluten free noodles.

VEGAN BASIL CREAM SAUCE

This is a sauce that will have you licking the bowl! I made it to have over gluten free noodles and veggies but it is good on grilled chicken, grilled veggies or even as a dip. The cream part comes from the soaked and blended raw cashews. If you have a batch of cashew cream in the fridge you can use that as the base and add the garlic, onion and basil to that.

For a tasty change try using this sauce in the chicken divine recipe instead of the cashew cream. Put a little of this sauce over fresh sliced ripe heirloom tomatoes for a burst of flavor also.

PREP: 10; COOK: SOAK 6 HOURS; SERVES: 1 CUP

Ingredients
- 1 cup raw whole cashews
- ⅔ cup water
- 1 teaspoon yellow onion, grated
- 2 cloves garlic minced
- 1 tablespoon fresh lemon juice
- ¾ cup packed fresh basil
- ½ teaspoon sea salt
- ⅛ teaspoon ground black pepper

1. Soak the raw cashews in a bowl of water for 6 hours or overnight.
2. Drain and rinse the cashews after they are done soaking.
3. In a powerful blender add the cashews, the water, grated onion, minced garlic, fresh lemon juice, basil, salt and black pepper. Blend until smooth. Taste for salt and pepper.

ZUCCHINI NOODLE LASAGNE

I use to love a good lasagne and always adored the left overs the next day. After becoming gluten, sugar and dairy free I wanted to create a version that was familiar flavor and texture. I found that using zucchini for the noodles and cashew cream in place of traditional ricotta cheese makes a delicious meal!

I also added thin slices of portobello mushrooms to ad more texture and depth to the dish. Feel free to use a home made marinara sauce or a good quality organic one. I used a little vegan mozzarella cheese in the middle of the layers and on the top to create that familiar texture and look. This dish turns out great every time and left overs are wonderful also.

PREP: 15; COOK: 60; SERVES: 4

Ingredients
- 2 large zucchini or 4 small
- 2 portabello mushrooms, gills removed
- 1 cup cashew cream
- 2 cups marinara sauce (or 1 jar marinara sauce)
- ½ cup vegan mozzarella cheese

1. Preheat oven to 350 degrees fahrenheit
2. Cut the ends off the zucchini squash and cut in half.
3. Using a mandolin or very sharp knife, thinly slice the squash into flat slices.
4. Using a spoon take the gills out of the portobello mushrooms.
5. Using a very sharp knife, thinly slice the mushroom into thin strips.
6. In the bottom of a baking dish, spoon ¼ cup of the marinara sauce into the dish and spread evenly.
7. Place a layer of the "zucchini" noodles down on the sauce. Top with ⅓ of the cashew cream.
8. Lay a layer of the mushroom slices and ⅓ of the marinara sauce.
9. Sprinkle ½ of the vegan mozzarella cheese over the sauce.

10. Place another layer of the zucchini slices, ⅓ of the cashew cream and then top with the rest of the mushroom slices.
11. Cover the mushrooms with all but 2 tablespoons of the marinara sauce and then a final layer of the zucchini noodles.
12. Mix the 2 tablespoons of the marinara sauce into the remaining ⅓ of the cashew cream and evenly coat the zucchini noodles.
13. Cover with foil and bake for 50 minutes.
14. Uncover and sprinkle with the other half of the vegan mozzarella cheese and bake for another 10 minutes.
15. Let sit 5 minutes before cutting.

Pork

Andouille Sausage, red beans and rice 80
Apple Cranberry Stuffed Pork Roast 81
Apple Roasted Pork Tenderloin 83
Ham and White Bean Soup 85
Roasted Pork Chops 86
Tuscan Pork 87

ANDOUILLE SAUSAGE, RED BEANS AND RICE

This classic dish popular in Louisiana comes with andouille sausage and is typically served over white rice. I normally serve mine over brown rice. Read the labels on the sausages, there are brands that are gluten free. I use a locally made one that is a chicken andouille. This recipe is written for the slow cooker. If using dried beans, soak over night and rinse. If using canned beans, drain and rinse first. This dish can be made stove top. In that case bring up to a bubble and then lower the heat to low and simmer for an hour.

prep: 10; cook 6-8 hrs; serves 4-6

Ingredients
- 1 red bell pepper, diced
- 1 yellow onion, diced
- 3 celery stalks, diced
- 5 garlic cloves, minced
- 4 andouille sausages, sliced (or one large one)
- 1 can fire roasted tomatoes
- 1 pound red kidney beans (that soaked over night and were rinsed)
- 6 cups water
- 2 teaspoons oregano
- 1 teaspoon thyme
- 3 teaspoons chili powder
- ½ teaspoon cayenne pepper
- ½ teaspoon cumin
- 1 teaspoon salt
- ½ teaspoon fresh black pepper

1. cooked rice, for serving
2. Put all the ingredients except for the rice into slow cooker and stir well.
3. Let cook on high 6 hours. Stir occasionally. Check to see if it needs to cook longer.
4. Note: Using soaked beans is better but if you use canned beans cook time would be less.
5. Note: You can use turkey or chicken sausage also.
6. Serve over cooked white rice.

APPLE CRANBERRY STUFFED PORK ROAST

This apple cranberry stuffed pork roast is a perfect fall dinner. It is easy to make but when you slice it and see all of the beautiful cooked apples and cranberries in the center, it has a huge wow factor. A easy family dinner or holiday dish to serve to guests.

SERVES 4; PREP 20; COOK 30

Ingredients
- 1 pork tenderloin, trimmed
- 1 apple - fuji, golden delicious, granny smith (your choice)
- 1 yellow onion
- 2 garlic cloves
- 1 tablespoon apple cider vinegar
- 4 teaspoons coconut oil divided
- 1 teaspoon fresh rosemary or ½ teaspoon dried
- ½ teaspoon salt
- fresh black pepper
- ⅔ cup chicken stock
- ⅓ cup apple cider
- 1½ tablespoons dijon mustard
- ⅓ cup dried cranberries

1. Pre heat oven to 425 degrees F.
2. Peel and core the apple and chop into small pieces and put into a bowl. Dice the onion and mince the garlic and add to the bowl with apples. Add the cranberries and toss well.
3. In a medium skillet over medium high heat, add 2 teaspoons of the coconut oil and let it melt.
4. Add the veggies from the bowl and sauté for 5 minutes as you stir.
5. Add the vinegar and fresh chopped rosemary and stir, cook for 1-2 minutes until apples are tender. Pour the veggie/fruit mix into a bowl.
6. Slice the port tenderloin lengthwise. Make sure not to cut all the way through but enough to open the piece of pork up enough for it to lay flat. You may need to make more than one cut to achieve this.
7. Cover the pork with plastic wrap and pound with a meat mallet or rolling pin so that it is all one thickness.

8. Sprinkle the salt and pepper over the outside and inside of the roast.
9. Spread the veggie/fruit mixture evenly over the inside of the pork. Carefully rollup the piece of pork making sure the stuffing stays inside.
10. Use cooking twine or tooth picks to keep the pork in its roll.
11. In a medium oven proof skillet melt the rest of the coconut oil over medium high heat.
12. Add the pork seam side down and let it brown. Carefully turn the pork until it is brown on all of the outside of the roll. 5-8 minutes total.
13. Put the skillet into the preheated oven for 15-20 minutes until it is done. Pork is done when a thermometer is inserted into the center and registers 145 degrees F.
14. Remove the pork from the pan and let stand 5-10 minutes so that the juices redistribute.
15. While the pork rests, put the pan back on the stove over medium high heat with all of the drippings of the roast.
16. Add the stock, cider and mustard. With a whisk scrape up any brown bits and bring to a boil. Taste for salt and pepper.
17. Note: I like to add a pinch of fresh finely chopped rosemary in this step.
18. Cook for 2-3 minutes.
19. Slice the pork into rounds and spoon the sauce over the pork when serving.

APPLE ROASTED PORK TENDERLOIN

Apples and pork are a classic and delicious combination and this roast is no exception. With the added tang of dijon mustard and the extra pop of apple cider, this dish goes from being ordinary to extraordinary! The meat comes out tender and tasty and the apples are a nice sweet compliment to the dish. Serve with my country style potatoes and the sweet pearl onions and peas. A meal that is delicious but beautiful!

PREP TIME: 10 MINUTES; COOK TIME: 35 MINUTES; SERVES: 2-3

Ingredients

- 1 large pork tenderloin (about 1½ pounds)
- 2 Apples (Granny Smith, Macintosh or Braeburn)
- 1 Tablespoon fresh thyme leaves
- 3 Tablespoons Dijon Mustard
- 1 Yellow Onion, sliced
- ½ Cup Apple cider
- 2 Tablespoons Coconut Oil
- 1½ Teaspoon Salt
- ½ Teaspoon fresh black pepper

1. Preheat oven to 425° Fahrenheit
2. Season the pork tenderloin all over with the 1 teaspoon of salt and the black pepper.
3. Peel, core and slice the apples into ¼ inch slices and put into a bow and add the sliced onions and toss to mix.
4. In a large skillet, add the coconut oil and let it melt over medium high heat. Then sear the pork on all sides until brown. About 5 minutes.
5. Remove the pork and put on a plate to cool.
6. Add the apple onion mixture to the skillet and sauté until the onions start to get soft about 3 minutes.
7. Put the onion mixture in a baking dish and add the apple cider and ½ teaspoon of salt and stir to mix.
8. Mix the mustard with the fresh thyme leaves and then rub all over the pork tenderloin.

Continued ➜

APPLE ROASTED PORK TENDERLOIN *Continued*

9. Place the tenderloin on top of the onion and apple mix and put into the oven.
10. Roast for 15-20 minutes and the meat thermometer registers 150° Fahrenheit
11. Transfer the pork to a platter and let sit for 5 minutes to redistribute the juices.
12. Slice the pork into ½ inch slices and pour the apple and onion mixture over the slices.

HAM AND WHITE BEAN SOUP

This is much hardier than a soup, this is a meal in a bowl. Packed full of wonderful white beans, chunks of ham, fire roasted tomato and small chunks of potato. It is a quick pull together if you use canned beans. I have a friend who loves this meal in a bowl with lots of hot sauce. However you doctor your bowl up, your appetite will be satisfied.

SERVES: 4 - 6; PREP: 10; COOK: 50

Ingredients
- 3 cans of white beans, rinsed and divided
- 1 small potato, peeled and diced
- 2 carrots, peeled and diced
- 1 yellow onion, minced
- 1 can fire roasted tomatoes
- 4 cloves of garlic, minced
- 4 cups of stock (vegetable or chicken)
- 1 pound ham steak (about 2 cups worth), cut into chunks
- 1 ham shank
- 1 teaspoon oregano
- ½ teaspoon basil
- 1 bay leaf
- ½ teaspoon salt
- 1 tablespoon coconut oil

1. Heat the coconut oil in a large soup pot over medium heat.
2. Add onion, carrot and potato and sauté for 10 min, adding the garlic the last minute.
3. Add the stock, chunks of ham, ham shank, seasonings and 2 cans of beans.
4. Bring up to a boil, lower to a simmer and partially cover for 30 minutes.
5. Take the last can of soup and mash until smooth, thick and creamy. Add to soup, stirring well to incorporate. Cook 10 more minutes.
6. Take out the ham shank and bay leaf before serving.

ROASTED PORK CHOPS

This is a nice, easy to make, hearty dish. The pork cooks perfectly and all of the flavors of the veggies and seasonings make you want to have second helpings! The nice thing about this dish is it is a one dish meal, cooks perfectly well together and you can add mushrooms or bell peppers to the veggie mix if you desire.

SERVES 4; PREP TIME 15; COOK TIME 60 MINUTES

Ingredients

- ½ teaspoon dried oregano leaves
- ½ teaspoon dried thyme leaves
- ½ teaspoon salt
- ½ teaspoon coarse ground pepper
- 4 pork rib chops, ½ inch thick (1 pound)
- small bag of red potatoes, about 3 cups quartered
- 3-4 carrots peeled and cut into 1 inch pieces
- 1 med yellow bell pepper cut into strips
- 2 medium onion,s cut into thin wedges
- 2 red tomatoes cut into wedges
- 1 head garlic peeled
- 2 tablespoons melted coconut oil

1. Pre heat oven to 400
2. In a large bowl mix the carrots, potatoes, bell pepper, onions, tomatoes and garlic. Add the coconut oil, salt, pepper, thyme and oregano and mix well.
3. Season the chops with salt and pepper on both sides.
4. Pour the veggie mix into the bottom of a baking dish. Lay the pork chops on top of the mixture.
5. Bake uncovered on the middle rack in the oven for 45 minutes.
6. Take the dish out of the oven, put the chops on a plate and mix the veggies. Then put the chops back on top of the veggies, the other side up.
7. Bake for another 15-20 minutes until the meat is at 145 degrees fahrenheit.
8. Pull the dish. Put the chops on a plate to rest for 3-5 minutes.
9. Stir the veggies before serving.

TUSCAN PORK

When I think of the flavors of Tuscany, I think of tomatoes, garlic, oregano and wine. This recipe blends those flavors together beautifully. The onions caramelize which adds a deep sweet note that blends nicely with the fire roasted tomatoes.

The pork chops are browned and then nestled in the flavorful sauce as they gently cook. This is so good that it could also be done with chicken or the sauce alone over gluten free pasta .

PREP: 10; COOK: 30-40; SERVES: 4

Ingredients
- 4 pork chops, fat trimmed
- 1 tbsp coconut oil
- 4 cloves of garlic, diced
- 1 can fire roasted tomatoes
- 1 large onion, finely diced
- 2 tsp oregano
- 1 tsp basil
- ½ tea salt
- ¼ tea pepper
- ¼ white wine

1. Heat a large skillet or Dutch oven on the stove over medium high heat.
2. Add the coconut oil and let it melt, coating the bottom of the pan.
3. Season the chops with a pinch of salt and pepper. Add to the pan and brown each side, about 3 minutes each side.
4. Remove chops from pan and set on plate to rest. (They are not done yet)
5. Reduce heat to medium-low, add onions. Stir onions and caramelize about 5 min they should be golden in color.
6. Add the tomatoes, garlic and spices. and wine to the pan and stir to mix.
7. Bring the sauce up to a bubble and then nestle pork chops in mix and lower heat to med low
8. Cover and simmer until pork chops are done 15-20 minutes
9. Remove the pork chips and plate, spooning sauce over each one.

Poultry

Baked Chicken and Mushrooms 90
Chicken Apple Stuffed Peppers 91
Chicken Bella 92
Chicken Cacciatore 93
Chicken Divan Casserole 95
Chicken Fajitas 96
Chicken Kabobs 97
Chipotle Chicken 99
Classic Roast Chicken 100
Creamy Mushroom Chicken 101
Crockpot Chicken Taco Chili 102
Easy Chicken Piccata 103
Gourmet Chicken Stroganoff 105
Grilled Mustard Chicken 107
Lemon Tarragon Chicken 108
Orange Roast Chicken Breasts 109
Roast Garlic Chicken 110
Slow Cooker White Chicken Chili 111
Spicy Chicken Legs 112
Spicy Honey Mustard Chicken Wings 114
Spinach and Mushroom
    Stuffed Chicken Breasts 115
Thai Chicken Skewers 116
Thai Mango Chicken Curry 117
Vinegar Chile Chicken Wings 119

BAKED CHICKEN AND MUSHROOMS

This baked chicken and mushrooms is not your old fashioned cream of mushroom soup and chicken, it goes way past that! The skin on the chicken is nice and crispy and is cooked in a creamy mushroom sauce flavored with thyme and garlic. It is so easy to make and yet amazing enough for company.

SERVE 4; PREP 15; COOK 60 MIN

Ingredients

- 4 bone in chicken breasts
- 3 cloves garlic, minced
- 8 ounces baby bella mushrooms cut in quarters
- ¼ yellow onion, minced
- ¾ cup chicken tock
- 2 tablespoons coconut oil
- 1 teaspoon thyme divided
- ½ teaspoon oregano
- ½ cup coconut milk
- 1 tablespoon dijon mustard
- ½ teaspoon salt divided
- black pepper to taste

1. Pre heat oven to 400 degrees
2. Season chicken breasts with salt, pepper and half of the thyme.
3. In large skillet heat the coconut oil over medium heat. Add the chicken skin side down and sear until golden brown about 4 minutes. Add the garlic, onion and mushrooms. Cook until browned about 6-8 minutes. Put on plate to wait.
4. Add the salt, pepper, thyme, oregano and mustard to the pan and stir well
5. Add the stock and coconut milk and bring up to heat stirring well. Once up to a boil. Turn off heat and add the chicken breasts skin side up. Cook in oven until done about 35-40 minutes.
6. Remove chicken to platter and cook the mushroom mixture until liquid is reduced for about 5 minutes. Taste for salt and pepper. Pour over chicken and serve.

CHICKEN APPLE STUFFED PEPPERS

Stuffed Peppers have become a favorite breakfast for me because they are easy to assemble and the oven does the work. A great way to get protein and veggies in me first thing in the morning.

SERVES 4; PREP 5; COOK 35

Ingredients
- 4 bell peppers, cut in half, seeded and deveined
- 8 eggs, beaten
- 1 package of chicken and apple sausage, diced
- 2 cups of spinach, chopped
- ½ cup salsa
- ½ teaspoon salt
- black pepper

1. Heat oven to 350 degrees F.
2. In a large bowl mix the chopped spinach and sausage together. Put ¼ of the mix into each half of bell pepper.
3. Put the salsa in the baking dish and put peppers stuffed side up, into the baking dish.
4. In a large bowl add the eggs, salt and peer and beat well.
5. Pour egg mixture into each bell pepper.
6. Bake in oven 25-35 minutes until set and done.

CHICKEN BELLA

This delicious chicken bella is flavored with baby bella mushrooms, garlic, turmeric and white wine. It creates a sauce that the rice or quinoa soaks up delightfully. The bell pepper and asparagus add a nice layer of flavor.

PREP: 20; SERVES 4-6; COOK 45

Ingredients

- 4 boneless skinless chicken breasts cut into bite size pieces
- 2 cups chicken stock
- ½ cup cashew cream
- 1 red bell pepper cut into bite size pieces
- 8 ounces baby bella mushrooms sliced
- ½ bunch baby asparagus cut into one inch pieces
- 1 small yellow onion, j sliced thin
- 2 cloves of garlic, minced
- 2 tablespoons coconut oil divided
- ¼ cup white wine
- 1 teaspoon turmeric
- ½ teaspoon oregano
- ¼ teaspoon salt
- fresh black pepper

1. Prep your veggies on one board and your chicken on another board. Pre heat oven to 350 degrees.
2. In a large skillet over medium high heat, melt the coconut oil. Add the veggies and sauté until the onion is translucent. Put in a large bowl to cool when done. In the same skillet add the second tablespoon of coconut oil and heat over medium high heat. Add the chicken pieces and cook until cooked through. Add to the same bowl with the veggies.
3. In the same skillet over medium high heat, add the chicken stock, white wine, the cashew cream, turmeric, oregano, salt and fresh black pepper. Once it comes to heat lower and simmer for 5 minutes. Add to the chicken and veggie mixture.
4. Pour the mixture into a casserole dish. You may cover it and cook it the next day or bake for 45 minutes uncovered in 350 degree oven.

CHICKEN CACCIATORE

This is a super easy dish to make that has wonderful flavor and turns out great every time. Even if this is your first time to make Chicken Cacciatore and you have guests coming over for dinner, do it! The sauce is full of flavor with all of the veggies and herbs. The one trick to the dish is to brown the chicken well on all sides before putting it into the sauce. The browning does two things: it gives the dish a deeper flavor and second it adds some nice crispy skin to the dish when serving. I love mushrooms in my dish but feel free to omit them if you choose. The capers are drained and add nice little pops of flavor.

If you make the dish the day before, it can be easily reheated in the oven covered. Once it is heated through, zest a little lemon over the dish. The lemon zest will wake up the veggie and tomato sauce.

SERVES: 4-6; PREP: 15; COOK: 45; EASY

Ingredients
- 1 chicken cut into pieces
- 2 teaspoons salt
- 1 teaspoon pepper
- 2 tablespoons coconut oil
- 1 red bell pepper sliced thin
- 1 yellow onion, sliced thin
- 8 ounces baby bella mushrooms sliced
- 4 cloves of garlic, minced
- ¾ cup white wine
- 1 can fire roasted tomatoes
- 1 cup chicken stock
- 3 tablespoons capers
- 1 teaspoon dried oregano
- 1 teaspoon dried basil
- handful fresh basil leaves, chopped

1. Preheat oven to 350 degrees
2. Sprinkle the chicken pieces with salt and pepper.
3. In a large deep oven proof skillet, melt the coconut oil.
4. Add the chicken and cook until golden brown, 5-6 minutes per side.
5. Put chicken on platter to sit.

Continued ➔

CHICKEN CACCIATORE *Continued*

6. Add the wine to the skillet and bring up to bubble. Then add the stock, capers, oregano, basil, tomatoes, garlic, onions, mushrooms and bell peppers. Cook for 10 minutes stirring well.
7. Add the chicken to the sauce, nestling the pieces into the sauce.
8. Put the skillet into the oven uncovered and roast until chicken is cooked through, the juices run clear when pierced with a knife, about 30 minutes. You may need to cook up to 45 minutes depending on your oven.
9. Serve the chicken with the sauce poured over it. Sprinkle with the chopped fresh basil.

CHICKEN DIVAN CASSEROLE

This recipe is my version of the classic chicken divan that was so popular in the 1960's and 1970's. The original dish was made with cream of chicken soup. mayo, sour cream and cheddar cheese. I replaced all of those ingredients with cashew cream and coconut milk. Then I added more flavor with lemon juice, madras curry powder and good white wine. The cashew cream thickens the sauce as it bakes in the oven. The result is a very tasty dish that is similar to the original but dairy free and much more healthy.

Yield: 4 Servings; Prep Time: 20 Minutes; Cook Time: 60 Minutes

Ingredients
- 2 large roasted chicken breasts
- 4 cups broccoli florets
- ½ coconut milk
- ½ cup cashew cream
- zest one lemon
- juice of one lemon
- ¼ white wine
- ¼ teaspoon black pepper
- ½ teaspoon salt
- 2 teaspoons madras curry powder
- sprinkle of salt and pepper

1. preheat oven to 350
2. Steam the broccoli until it is just fork tender. Put on a platter. Sprinkle with salt and pepper. Let cool.
3. Dice the chicken breasts into cubes.
4. In a large bowl mix the coconut milk, cashew cream, lemon zest, lemon juice, white wine, black pepper, sea salt and madras curry powder.
5. Add the cooled broccoli and cubed chicken to the sauce. Stir gently until everything is coated in the sauce.
6. Pour into a small baking dish using your spatula to flatten out the top of the casserole.
7. Cover tightly with foil.
8. Bake for 30 minutes covered and another 30 minutes uncovered.
9. Let sit for 5 minutes so that the sauce can settle. Enjoy!

CHICKEN FAJITAS

Chicken fajitas is a quick dish that is very easy to make and has tons of flavor. I love eating mine in butter lettuce leaves but corn tortillas work great also. I also like to use red, yellow and orange bell peppers since they add a lot of color, nutrients and are much sweeter than green bell peppers. Add some fresh salsa or some guacamole and you have a feast on your hands!

PREP 20; COOK 15; SERVES 4-6

Ingredients
- 2 pounds of chicken breasts, cut into strips
- 3 bell peppers
- 2 onions
- 2 teaspoons oregano
- 2 teaspoons chili powder
- 2 teaspoons cumin
- 3 cloves of garlic, minced
- 2 lemons, juiced
- 1 lime, juiced
- 1 jalapeño, seeded and minced
- 1 tablespoon coconut oil
- 1 bunch of cilantro

1. Take ¼ of the bunch of cilantro and chop the leaves, removing the stems and set aside.
2. In a blender add the rest of the cilantro (stems included), oregano, chili powder, cumin, garlic, lemon juice, lime juice and the jalapeño. Blend until smooth.
3. Cut the chicken into strips.
4. Seed and cut the bell peppers into strips.
5. Slice the onions into strips.
6. In a large bowl, combine the chicken, peppers, onions and the mixture from the blender and mix well. Cover and put in fridge for 2-4 hours.
7. In a large frying pan, heat the coconut oil.
8. Add the chicken mixture to the pan. Cook making sure to stir and turn the ingredients over in the pan. Cook for 6-9 minutes or until done.
9. Sprinkle the chopped, reserved cilantro over the chicken.
10. Serve with butter lettuce leaves or corn tortillas.

CHICKEN KABOBS

I love making chicken kabobs! It is a quick easy way to have dinner on the table quickly and it is a lot of fun. The best advice I can give you whenever you are making any type of kabobs; chicken, steak, shrimp or fish, is to do the protein on their own skewers and the veggies on their own. I know it looks pretty to have the veggies sprinkled among the protein pieces but veggies and the proteins have different cooking times.

You can marinade the veggies in the same marinade as the protein or you can follow my Roasted Balsamic Veggie recipe. Either way, make sure to separate the protein and the veggies. I always make double batches of the roasted veggies because they are great as a side dish the following night!

There are so many different marinades that you can put on grilled chicken kabobs. In fact you could make a different flavored chicken kabob every night of the week!

I personally generally use metal skewers but if you are going to use bamboo skewers, soak them in water for 1 hour before grilling to protect them from burning on the grill.

SERVES 4-6; PREP 10; COOK 8-10 MINUTES

Ingredients
- 2 pounds boneless, skinless chicken breasts
- 2 lemons, juiced
- 1 orange, juiced
- 1 lime, juiced
- 4 garlic cloves, minced
- 1/3 cup tamari, coconut amino or gluten free soy sauce
- 2 teaspoons honey (may omit if sensitive)

1. In a large bowl mix all the ingredients except for the chicken with a whisk until well incorporated. Set aside.
2. Cut the chicken breasts into large size cubes.

Continued ➜

CHICKEN KABOBS *Continued*

3. Add the chicken to the bowl of marinade and mix well. Cover with plastic wrap or put in large zip bag and put into the fridge.
4. Let the chicken marinate for 3 hours or overnight.
5. Note: If using same marinade for veggies, separate some in a separate bowl to marinate separately. Do not put raw chicken and veggies together.
6. Pre heat your grill to 375 degrees (a medium hot fire).
7. Skewer the chicken pieces allowing them to lightly touch but not compacting them tightly together.
8. Cook chicken until tender and cooked through, 8-10 minutes turning to make sure all sides are cooked.

Note: To cook skewers in oven: Heat to 425 F. Arrange skewers on baking sheet in single layer and cook 10-12 minutes.

CHIPOTLE CHICKEN

A chipotle is a smoked jalapeño that comes in a small can in adobo sauce. This simple ingredient can transform a dish with its smokey spicy notes. This dish calls for a sauce made with the chipotle in adobo sauce, tomato sauce, onions, cumin, garlic and chili powder. It is an easy one dish meal that has a lot of flavor.

SERVES 4; PREP TIME 5 MIN; COOK TIME 25

Ingredients

- 4 boneless skinless chicken breast halves
- 2 teaspoons cumin, divided
- ½ teaspoon chili powder
- 1 teaspoon salt, divided
- ¼ teaspoon pepper
- ½ to 1 medium chipotle chile in adobo sauce, minced
- 2 teaspoons adobo sauce
- 2 garlic cloves, minced
- ½ onion thinly sliced
- ½ cup tomato sauce
- 4 tablespoons chopped fresh cilantro, divided
- 2 teaspoons coconut oil
- 2 roma tomatoes

1. Combine 1 teaspoon cumin, chili powder and salt in small bowl and then sprinkle over chicken on both sides.
2. Combine chipotle chile, adobo sauce, minced garlic, sliced onion, tomato sauce, roma tomatoes, 1 teaspoon cumin and ½ teaspoon salt into a small pan and let simmer over medium heat for 10 minutes. Tasting sauce for salt and pepper.
3. Heat coconut oil in large nonstick skillet over medium-high heat until it melts, coating the bottom of the skillet.
4. Add seasoned chicken breasts to pan making sure not to over lap.
5. Cook chicken 4 minutes or until browned on one side.
6. Turn chicken breasts over and top with the tomato sauce mixture.
7. Reduce heat to medium-low; simmer, covered, 10-15 minutes or until chicken is no longer pink in center.
8. Remove from heat. Stir 3 tablespoons of the cilantro into sauce.
9. Serve chicken with sauce over it and top with remaining cilantro.

CLASSIC ROAST CHICKEN

One of the most classic Sunday family dinners is roast chicken. This dish has all of the same flavors and aromas but in a single serving. Make sure you use a chicken breast that has the bone in, it adds a lot of flavor. I love the smell of garlic and rosemary in the air as it cooks. I also like to roast a few extra breasts for salads and sandwiches the next day. By cooking it this way, the breast soaks up a lot of flavor.

PREP TIME: 5 MIN.; MARINADE TIME: 1 HOUR; COOK TIME: 90 MIN.; SERVES: 4

Ingredients
- 1 chicken
- 2 lemons juiced
- 5 garlic cloves smashed
- 2 sprig fresh rosemary
- 6-8 sprigs thyme
- ¼ cup olive oil
- ¼ teaspoon salt
- ¼ teaspoon black pepper

1. Pre Heat Oven 350 degrees
2. Wash and dry chicken leaving skin intact. Place in a plastic zip bag.
3. In a bowl mix the lemon juice, smashed garlic cloves, rosemary, olive oil, salt and pepper. Pour over chicken breast in plastic bag and seal. Refrigerate for 1 hour, turning the bag over once after 30 minutes.
4. Remove chicken from marinade and place on a baking sheet or a rack in a baking dish. Bake 350° for 90 minutes. The chicken is done when the juices run clear or it reaches 165° internally.
5. Serving Suggestion: If fresh rosemary is not available use ½ teaspoon dried rosemary. Cooking the chicken on the bone keeps the breast juicy and gives more flavor. For a more intense lemon flavor zest the lemon and add the zest to the marinade.

CREAMY MUSHROOM CHICKEN

This is a very easy delicious dinner that is also perfect for company. It comes out fantastic every time! I love creamy mushroom sauce and chicken but I did not want to stand over the stove the entire time.

So I adapted my chicken and mushroom dish that use to use boneless chicken breast browned and then covered with a mushroom sauce I made on the stove top using cream.

This new version has much more flavor and actually has a much deeper flavor since the bone in chicken is cooked tight on top of the mushrooms and other ingredients as they all cook together. Enjoy!

PREP TIME 10; COOK TIME 60; SERVES 4

Ingredients

- 4 bone in chicken breasts
- 3 cloves garlic, minced
- 8 ounces cremini mushrooms, halved
- ¾ cup chicken stock
- ¾ teaspoon dried thyme
- ½ tea salt
- ¼ tea black pepper
- ½ cup coconut milk
- 1 tablespoon dijon mustard

1. Preheat oven to 350 degrees F. S
2. Season chicken breasts with a pinch of salt and pepper.
3. In a large bowl add the garlic, mushrooms, chicken stock, salt, pepper, coconut milk and mustard. Mix well making sure that all the ingredients are incorporated.
4. Put the mushroom mixture on the bottom of a baking dish. Place the chicken breasts on top. Bake for one hour.
5. Pull the chicken out of the sauce, set aside and cover to keep warm.
6. Stir the mushroom sauce, if it is too thin, pour the mushroom mixture in a sauce pan and cook for about 5-10 minutes over medium heat until thickens more.
7. Plate the chicken and pour the sauce over.

CROCKPOT CHICKEN TACO CHILI

When I lived in New Mexico as a girl I use to love to ski and would go up the mountain any chance I could. I would come home to a big pot of beef chili and beans cooking on the stove after a long day of skiing. I loved how the house smelled and eagerly looked forward to a huge bowl of it. Now back then I would eat bowls of it!

This is my version of that chili using chicken and green chilies. I love green chilies and I order 20 pounds of them every year from Hatch New Mexico. I roast them and put them in the freezer. The canned ones work fine for this recipe.

Make sure to shred the chicken meat half an hour or more before serving and let it soak up all the flavors of the sauce during that time. You will want bowls of this chili.

SERVES 4-6; PREP 10; COOK 6 HRS

Ingredients

- 4 skinless boneless chicken breasts
- 1 onion, finely chopped
- 1 16-oz can kidney beans rinsed
- 1 can fire roasted green chili
- 2 cans fire roasted tomatoes
- 2 tbsp cumin
- 2 tbsp chili powder
- ½ tea oregano
- ½ tea salt
- ¼ tea pepper
- ¼ cup chopped fresh cilantro (garnish)
- ½ finely diced onion (garnish)

1. Combine beans, onion, green chilies, fire roasted tomatoes and the seasonings in to a crock pot. Stir well.
2. Place chicken breasts on top of mixture and cover.
3. Cook on low for 8-10 hours or on high for 4-5 hours.
4. Half hour before serving, remove chicken and shred using two forks.
5. Return chicken to slow cooker and mix into the veggie mix, cover and cook 30 more min.
6. Top with fresh cilantro and onions.

EASY CHICKEN PICCATA

I loved chicken piccata when I discovered it in my 20's. I was working on a mental health forensic team at the time and we would go out to dinner once a month at this Italian restaurant. I ordered the chicken piccata and it came with steamed broccoli and roasted red potatoes. I loved that butter, lemon, caper sauce so much that I would have the chef put extra over my broccoli and potatoes. I was addicted to it. I ordered that same dish every single month for a few years. Then the restaurant was closing and the chef taught me how easy it was to make the lemon sauce. This is my GSDF version of that same dish.

SERVES: 4; PREP TIME: 15; COOK: 20

Ingredients
- 1 Lb. of chicken tenders
- 1 lemon
- 2 Tbsp. Coconut oil
- 1-cup coconut flour or gluten free flour mix
- ⅓ cup lemon juice (1-2 lemons)
- ½ cup chicken stock
- 3 Tbsp. capers
- 2 Tbsp. chopped parsley
- Salt
- Pepper

1. Heat coconut oil in large frying pan over medium heat.
2. Sprinkle some salt and pepper over the chicken tenders.
3. Dredge the tenders in flour and shaking off the excess.
4. Juice the lemons.
5. Add the chicken to the skillet not crowding it and doing it in two batches.
6. When the side is brown flip and cook other side about 5 minutes total.
7. Remove from the pan and put on plate covered with foil to keep warm.
8. Do the second batch of chicken tenders.
9. In the pan add the lemon juice, stock and capers.

Continued ➤

EASY CHICKEN PICCATA *Continued*

10. Stir and scrape up any brown bits. Cook over low heat at a simmer for 5 min.
11. Add the chicken back to the pan to warm through. 2-3 minutes.
12. Serve the chicken pouring the sauce over the chicken and topping with chopped parsley.

POULTRY

GOURMET CHICKEN STROGANOFF

My happy place is in recipe creation, food flavor profiles and in the kitchen. So after a stressful day, I had a craving for a big bowl of beef stroganoff. I decided to indulge my desire and create a gluten dairy free version that would still taste delicious, be comforting and enjoyable. When I went to the kitchen to crate my new dish, I only had chicken on hand. So my gourmet chicken stroganoff was created.

PREP TIME: 10 MINUTES; COOK TIME: 35 MINUTES; YIELD: 4 SERVINGS

Ingredients

- 3 tablespoons coconut oil divided
- 1 small yellow onion or half of a normal one diced
- 1-2 diced cloves of garlic
- 4-5 fresh shiitake mushrooms sliced
- ⅓ cup of diced chanterelle mushrooms
- ½ cup good white wine
- ½ cup good chicken stock
- 1¼ cup coconut milk
- ½ teaspoon thyme
- ½ teaspoon salt
- ¼ teaspoon fresh ground black pepper
- 1 large boneless skinless chicken breast or 2 normal size ones sliced
- 1 package gluten free pasta cooked

1. Heat 2 tablespoons of coconut oil in a large skillet on medium heat. Add the diced onions and garlic and sautŽ until translucent.
2. Add the sliced and diced mushrooms and cook until mushrooms are tender. Cook for about 3 minutes.
3. Add the white wine and cook 2-3 minutes until the wine is almost completely evaporated.
4. Add the stock, coconut milk, thyme, salt and pepper.
5. In another small frying pan, add the coconut oil and cook over medium heat the strips of chicken breast until done. This takes about 2 minutes a side.

Continued ➤

GOURMET CHICKEN STROGANOFF *Continued*

6. Add the cooked chicken to the sauce. Bring up to a boil and then lower to simmer for 10 minutes stirring occasionally. The sauce will thicken naturally
7. Add the cooked pasta to the sauce and mix well. Let cook together for 2 minutes so that the noodles soak up the flavorful sauce.

GRILLED MUSTARD CHICKEN

Grilled Mustard Chicken was created one evening with ingredients I had on hand. It has now become one of my favorite chicken dishes. I really enjoy cooking with Dijon mustard, it adds a lot of flavor to a dish. I always have chicken breasts in the freezer. They only take about 20 minutes to thaw if you put them in a zip bag in a bowl of water. So, sometimes when I am hungry I quickly thaw a chicken breast.

PREP TIME: 5 MINUTES; COOK TIME: 10 MINUTES; SERVES: 4

Ingredients
- 4 tablespoons Dijon mustard
- 4 tablespoons white wine
- 2 tablespoons coarse mustard
- 1½ - 2 teaspoons hot sauce
- 3 tablespoons honey
- 4 tablespoons olive oil
- 4 cloves of garlic chopped

1. Whisk all the ingredients except the chicken breast together in a bowl. Whisk until the marinade emulsifies.
2. Place in a large zip bag. Add the chicken and make sure the sauce coats all sides.
3. Place the bag in the refrigerator for at least 30 minutes. Turning the bag once for equal coating.
4. Grill chicken breast 4-5 minutes on each side. The internal temperature should be 160°.
5. Serving Suggestions: This dish can be baked if preferred.

LEMON TARRAGON CHICKEN

This lemon tarragon chicken recipe was created after I returned home from the Farmer's Market with a fresh bundle of tarragon. I loved the smell and the flavor. Tarragon is actually a species of perennial herb in the sunflower family. It adds a distinctive flavor to the dish almost like that of anise or licorice.

SERVES 4; PREP 15; COOK 60

Ingredients
- 4 skinless bone-in chicken breasts
- 2 tablespoons olive oil
- 4 tablespoons tarragon leaves
- ½ Tsp. salt
- ¼ Tsp. ground pepper
- 2 onions, peeled, halved and sliced into half rings
- 2 cups gluten-free low-sodium chicken broth
- 2 lemons, juiced

1. Preheat oven to 350°F
2. Toss chicken pieces with olive oil and half the tarragon leaves.
3. Season liberally with salt and pepper and toss well to make sure all pieces are evenly coated.
4. Arrange onion slices in the bottom of a baking pan or oven-proof Dutch oven large enough to hold chicken pieces as best as possible in one layer.
5. Sprinkle remaining half of tarragon leaves over onions and arrange chicken on top.
6. Add chicken broth and lemon juice, cover place in the oven.
7. Bake for about an hour or until juices run clear when chicken pieces are pierced with a fork.
8. Remove from oven, covered, and let rest 10 minutes.
9. Just before serving, taste the juices at the bottom of the pan and adjust seasoning with salt and pepper.
10. Serve chicken with juices spooned over it.

ORANGE ROAST CHICKEN BREASTS

These orange roast chicken breasts are delicious! The zest and juice of fresh oranges, honey, rosemary and a touch of spice make them really become the star of the plate. The honey also caramelizes while cooking so the skin gets really nice and crispy.

serves 4-6; prep 10 min; cook 60 min

Ingredients
- 5 tablespoons raw organic honey
- zest of 2 oranges
- juice of 2 oranges
- 6 tablespoons rosemary leaves chopped
- 1 tablespoon salt
- 2 teaspoons red pepper flakes
- 3/4 teaspoon freshly ground black pepper
- 4 chicken breasts or one chicken divided

1. Heat oven to 350 degrees F and arrange rack in middle.
2. In a large bowl, mix together honey, orange juice, orange zest, rosemary, salt, red pepper flakes, and freshly ground black pepper. Add chicken pieces and turn to coat well. Marinate 1 hour or up to over night.
3. Pull chicken out of marinade and put into a baking dish or on a sheet tray and bake for 50 minutes to one hour until done.

ROAST GARLIC CHICKEN

This roast garlic chicken was created one day when I was craving the 40 clove chicken from a restaurant in San Francisco called the Stinky Rose. They specialize in dishes with garlic. Their 40 clove chicken is divine. So this is my version of that dish. The chicken comes out moist, with crispy skin and flavored by not only the garlic but the fresh herbs.

Ingredients

- 1 whole chicken cut into pieces
- ½ Tsp. salt
- ¼ Tsp. black pepper
- 3 Tbsp. coconut oil
- 3 sprigs of parsley
- 5 sprigs of thyme
- 1 sprig of rosemary
- 1 whole head of garlic peeled
- ½ cup good white wine (stock can be substituted)

1. Heat oven to 350 degrees.
2. In large frying pan heat coconut oil.
3. Rinse chicken under cold water and dry .
4. Sprinkle chicken pieces with salt and pepper.
5. Place in frying pan to brown on each side taking care not to crowd the pan about 10 minutes
6. Tie herbs together with kitchen string (note if you don't have fresh herbs see note below recipe)*
7. In the bottom of a baking dish place the garlic cloves and the herbs.
8. Place chicken pieces on top of garlic, skin side up do not cover
9. Bake in oven 1 hour 20 minutes (until juices run clear)
10. Baste the chicken twice for best flavor
11. When done put chicken on plate to rest
12. Pour sauce and garlic cloves over chicken pieces

*__Note:__ If you don't have fresh herbs, even though they are best in this recipe do this: ¼ tea thyme ¼ tea rosemary Mix the dried herbs and sprinkle over chicken pieces before baking.

SLOW COOKER WHITE CHICKEN CHILI

A perfect healthy comfort dinner waiting for you when you get home when you use the slow cooker. This is a very easy dish to make but it has a wonderful layer of tasty flavors. I added a little of Southwestern flavor by using cumin, green chilies and cilantro. This is such an easy dish, all you have to do is add the ingredients and turn on your slow cooker. You will come home to a house full of delicious smells and warm bowls of mouth watering deliciousness!

Serves 6 to 8; prep: 15; Cook: 4-6 hours

Ingredients

- 4 boneless, skinless chicken breasts, cut into large chunks
- 1 yellow onion, diced
- 1 can diced fire roasted green chili peppers
- 4 cloves garlic, minced
- 2 teaspoons chili powder
- 1 teaspoons cumin
- 1 teaspoon salt
- ¼ teaspoon black pepper
- 1 teaspoon dried oregano
- 4 cups low-sodium chicken stock
- 1 can cannelloni , drained and rinsed
- ½ bunch cilantro, chopped

1. Combine the chicken, onions, green chili, garlic, cumin, chili powder, salt, oregano, black pepper, beans and stock in a 6-quart slow cooker.
2. Stir everything to mix well.
3. Place the lid on the slow cooker. Cook for 4 hours on high or 6 hours on low.
4. Serve in large bowls topped with the fresh cilantro.

Note: A squeeze of fresh lime is also delicious once cooked.

SPICY CHICKEN LEGS

Sometimes you just need some nice spicy chicken legs for dinner, then this is the recipe for you! This recipe calls for the use of a grill pan and the oven so that you get a great char on the legs before they finish baking. You can also just grill the legs on the outside BBQ. This is a great dish to make for football Sunday's in front of the game instead of chicken wings. Though this marinade is great also on chicken wings.

SERVES: 4; PREP: 10; COOKS: 20

Ingredients
- 4 whole skin on chicken legs
- ¼ cup rice vinegar
- 2 oranges
- 2 tablespoons Sriracha
- 3 cloves of garlic, minced
- 2 tablespoons tamari or coconut aminos
- 2 tablespoons organic raw honey
- 1 teaspoon red pepper flakes
- 2 tablespoons olive oil
- 1 tablespoon coconut oil
- ½ teaspoon salt
- fresh black pepper

1. Pre Heat oven to 400 degrees F.
2. Zest and juice one of the oranges, cut the other orange into 4 wedges.
3. In a large bowl, whisk together the rice vinegar, orange juice, orange zest, Sriracha, garlic, coconut aminos, honey, red pepper flakes, olive oil, salt and pepper.
4. Add the chicken legs and marinate for 30 minutes to two hours. I usually turn the legs over half way through or pour it all in a large zip bag.

Note: If you marinate the chicken over night, let it come up to room temperature before cooking because the honey gets a little hard in the fridge.

1. Heat a grill pan over medium heat and brush with a little coconut oil.
2. Remove the chicken from the marinade and place on the grill pan.
3. Cook each side 4-5 minutes each so that it gets a nice char.
4. Place pan into oven and bake for 10-15 minutes. The internal temperature of the chicken should be 165 degrees F.
5. Serve the chicken legs with a squeeze of the orange wedge over it.

SPICY HONEY MUSTARD CHICKEN WINGS

These wings disappeared from the plate Thursday night while watching pre-season football! They are a little messy but worth the mess! They come out spicy, tangy, sweet and delicious. Chicken wings and football is one of my favorite combinations so I like a variety of wings. This one is a sure winner.

SERVES:4; COOK: 40; PREP: 10

Ingredients

- 2 pounds chicken wings, flats and drummy seperated
- ½ cup local raw organic honey
- ⅓ cup Dijon mustard
- 2 tablespoons bourbon
- 1½ tablespoons tamari or coconut aminos
- ½ teaspoon red pepper flakes
- ¼ teaspoon salt
- 2 teaspoons sriracha (add more for more heat)
- 1½ tablespoons coconut oil

1. Pre heat oven to 400 degrees F.
2. In a medium size sauce pan, add all the ingredients and simmer while constantly stirring for 3 minutes.
3. Put the wings on a cooling rack on top of a large baking sheet. Spreading them out so that the air can circulate around them.
4. Put into oven cook 20 minutes, flip them over and another 20 minutes. they should be nice and golden.
5. You can put them under the broiler at this point for a few moments to make them a little more crispy.

SPINACH AND MUSHROOM STUFFED CHICKEN BREASTS

When I first wrote my recipe for stuffed chicken breasts it was for my cookbook: Family Favorites for One. I had used spinach, mushrooms, provolone cheese and a ton of wine. This is my easier version that still has the same flavor profile and is easy to make.

SERVES: 4; COOK TIME: 20; PREP: 15

Ingredients
- 4 boneless skinless chicken breasts
- 2 cups fresh spinach
- 2 garlic cloves, minced
- 1 cup crimini mushrooms, finely chopped
- 3 tablespoons coconut oil
- ¼ yellow onion, diced
- ½ teaspoon red pepper flakes
- ½ teaspoon salt
- fresh ground pepper
- ¼ cup white wine
- ½ cup chicken stock

1. In a large dry skillet, cook the spinach until wilted and sprinkle with a pinch of salt. Squeeze out the water and add to a bowl.
2. In a large skillet melt 1 tablespoon of the coconut oil.
3. Add to the skillet the onion, garlic and mushrooms. Cook for about 3-5 minutes over medium heat until done. Add to the spinach.
4. Once the spinach mixture has cooled mix ingredients well. Cut a horizontal slit through the chicken to create a pocket
5. Divide the spinach mix in half and stuff each breast and close the pockets with toothpicks.
6. Sprinkle the breasts with the salt, red pepper flakes and pepper evenly on both sides.
7. Add the 2 tablespoons of coconut oil to the skillet over medium heat.
8. Add the chicken breasts. Cook 4 minutes and then turn over. Add the wine and stock mix to the pan. Cover and cook 5 minutes.
9. Remove the lid and cook another 2-4 minutes until chicken is done and sauce is reduced.
10. Serve chicken with sauce poured over.

THAI CHICKEN SKEWERS

These Thai Chicken Skewers have so much flavor that you can eat them as is but they are also very good dipped into the Thai Inspired Almond Nut Sauce.

Serves: 10; Prep: 10; Cook: 5-7

Ingredients
- 2 pounds of chicken breast cut into strips (or use chicken tender pieces)
- ½ cup coconut aminos
- 4 tablespoons fresh lime juice
- 4 teaspoons fresh grated ginger
- 1 1/12 teaspoons red chili flakes
- 8-10 green onions chopped into 1 inch pieces (using the white and green parts)
- 1 teaspoon gram marsala curry powder

1. Mix all the ingredients except the chicken in a large plastic zip bag. If you want a little more marinade add a little water.
2. Once mixed, add the chicken strips and place in fridge.
3. Marinate 4 hours to overnight. This allows the flavor to go deep into the chicken.
4. **BBQ:** Place the strips on a well heated BBQ, turning once. Takes about 3-4 minutes per strip. Make sure you cook the chicken all the way through.
5. **STOVE TOP:** Heat a non-stick frying pan over medium heat and cook the strips turning once.

THAI MANGO CHICKEN CURRY

This is one of my favorite dishes to make when I find nice ripe mango at the market. I wrote it for 2 servings but it doubles and triples very well. This dish has a little bit of heat and a touch of sweet. I usually serve this over brown rice or quinoa. I like to use chicken stock instead of water when making rice or quinoa so it has a lot more flavor.

In most Thai curry dishes you put equal amounts of fish sauce and sugar. This dish did not need sugar because the mango was so ripe and sweet. If your mango is not as sweet feel free to add a little coconut sugar to the recipe.

I start the curry with the chicken stock, coconut milk, fish sauce and red curry paste over medium heat in a sauce pan. While the curry paste is melting into the liquid, I prepare the other ingredients. Cut the chicken into pieces, dice the bell pepper and dice the mango.

When chopping a mango there is an easier way! Cut the large sides off using your knife following along the smooth side of the large flat pit. Once the mango is cut off the seed, use a large spoon to scoop the meat out from the thick peel in one piece. Now you can chop the mango into similar pieces. Do this for each side.

SERVES 2; PREP: 10; COOK: 30

Ingredients
- 1 large or 2 small chicken breasts
- 1 large ripe mango
- 1 tablespoon fish sauce
- 1-2 teaspoons red curry paste (the more, the spicier)
- ½ red bell pepper diced
- ¾ cup coconut milk
- ¾ cup chicken stock
- 1 tablespoon chopped cilantro

1. Stir together the chicken stock, coconut milk, fish sauce and red curry paste over medium heat in a sauce pan and bring up to heat. Then let it simmer as the curry paste incorporates into the liquid, stirring occasionally.

Continued ➜

THAI MANGO CHICKEN CURRY *Continued*

2. Cut the chicken into 2-inch pieces.
3. Dice the bell pepper.
4. When chopping a mango there is an easier way! Cut the large sides off using your knife following along the smooth side of the large flat pit. Once the mango is cut off the seed, use a large spoon to scoop the meat out from the thick peel in one piece. Now you can chop the mango into similar pieces. Do this for each side and then dice the mango.
5. Once the red curry paste has integrated into the stock, add the mango, chicken and bell pepper.
6. Bring it up to a boil and immediately lower the heat to simmer for 20 minutes.
7. Once the curry is done, serve over your favorite brown rice or quinoa and sprinkle the chopped cilantro over the top of the dish.

VINEGAR CHILE CHICKEN WINGS

These chicken wings turn out sweet, spicy and tangy. Marinade them over night for the best flavor. You can either grill them the next day or bake them in the oven. These wings are a great snack on game day! Even cold the next day they are wonderful.

SERVES 4; PREP 10; COOK: 45

Ingredients

- 2 pounds chicken wings, tips removed and flats and drumettes separated
- ½ cup rice vinegar
- 2 tablespoons coconut oil
- 7 cloves of garlic, smashed
- 1 teaspoon red chili flakes
- 1 tablespoon honey
- 1 teaspoon salt
- 2 limes
- 2 teaspoons cumin
- 1 teaspoon hot chili powder

1. In a large zip plastic bag add the chilies, vinegar, coconut oil, garlic and salt to the bag. Shake to mix well.
2. Add the chicken wings to the bag and make sure every one gets coated with the marinade. Set in fridge over night.
3. Pre heat oven to 375 f or the bbq.
4. Remove wings from bag and pat dry.
5. in a bowl add 1 tablespoon coconut oil, cumin and chili powder, mix well.
6. Toss the wings in this mix and either bbq or lay on baking racks on baking sheets.
7. If cooking on BBQ: cook 15-20 minutes turning half way through.
8. If cooking in oven: bake 40-45 minutes turning half way through.
9. Plate and then zest the zest of one lime over the wings and squeeze the juice of both limes over the wings.
10. Serve and enjoy!

Salad

Beet Orange Salad 122
Best Cobb Salad... 123
Curry Chicken Salad...................................... 125
German Potato Salad 126
Green Papaya Salad 127
Grilled Caesar Salad 128
Grilled Chicken Asian Salad 129
Lemony Quinoa Tabouli 130
Lentil Salad... 131
Seaweed Salad 133
Spicy Thai Steak Salad 134
Sugar Snap Pea Salad 135
Sweet Potato Salad with Fresh Dill 136
Tomato Avocado Salad................................. 137

BEET AND ORANGE SALAD

This beet and orange salad is delicious. I love the flavor of roasted beets with the bright flavor citrus and the nice crunch of the chopped walnuts. It is actually very easy to make.

SERVES 4; COOK: 60 MIN; PREP: 10

Ingredients
- 1 pound of beets, greens cut off
- 3 oranges
- 3 tablespoons olive oil
- ¼ cup chopped walnuts
- pinch of salt

1. Preheat oven to 400 degrees F
2. Wash the beets and cut the leaves off.
3. Place large piece of foil on baking sheet. Put the beets in the middle and add 1 tablespoon of olive oil and 2 tablespoons water. Close the packet and roast one hour.
4. Juice one orange and put into a large bowl.
5. Add 2 tablespoons olive oil and a pinch of salt and mix well with a fork.
6. Segment the other two oranges and cut into pieces and add to the dressing.
7. Remove the beets from the oven let cool. Then peel and cut into wedges, add to the bowl.
8. Mix well, plate and sprinkle with chopped walnuts.

SALAD

BEST COBB SALAD

I love a good Cobb salad. I had a delicious one when I was traveling not long ago and it awakened the Cobb salad beast in me. Since I am dairy, gluten and sugar free, I no longer have the chunks of blue cheese on top. I also don't have the mounds of blue cheese dressing either. I got busy in my kitchen coming up with a way to get the creaminess and the decadence of the salad. I succeeded!

This is a filling salad with a lot of texture and flavor. Some people like to put hardboiled egg in the salad, feel free to do that. I always put the avocado next to the chicken and the bacon next, then the tomato. That way my bite has all of the ingredients in it! Enjoy!

Ingredients
- 1 boneless skinless chicken
- 1 tablespoon coconut oil
- 1 head of romaine lettuce
- 1 vine ripened tomato
- 2 slices of thick bacon
- ½ ripe avocado
- ¼ cups julienned carrots
- ¼ cup shredded purple cabbage
- ¼-⅓ cup of my delicious Ranch Dressing
- ⅛ teaspoon salt
- ⅛ teaspoon black pepper
- ¼ teaspoon herbs de Provence

1. Season the chicken breast with salt, pepper and herbs de provence on both sides.
2. Heat a small skillet with the coconut oil and cook the chicken until it is cooked through about
3. Chop into chunks and let cool.
4. Pre-heat the oven to 400°.
5. Cover a baking sheet with foil and place 2 pieces of bacon on it not touching. By cooking your bacon in the oven this way, it cooks flat and evenly.
6. Cook bacon for 11-14 minutes depending on your oven.

Continued ➤

BEST COBB SALAD *Continued*

7. Let cool on a paper towel covered plate to remove any excess oil.
8. Cut the lettuce into bite size pieces and toss with the carrots and cabbage and place in bottom of the serving bowl.
9. Next make rows of the other ingredients: diced avocado, chopped chicken breast, chopped bacon and diced tomatoes.
10. When you are ready to eat, drizzle the dressing over your salad.

SALAD

CURRY CHICKEN SALAD

Curry chicken salad is one of my favorite dishes to have on hand for quick lunches. I normally make it with apples and celery in it. It is also great with nuts (toasted almond slivers or cashews), raisins or died cherries.

I like to use a curry blend that is easy to find and it is called Madras Hot Curry Powder. I don't know why they call it hot because it is not spicy. The blend has fenugreek, coriander, cumin, turmeric, red bell pepper and garlic in it.

SERVES 4; COOK: 40-50 MIN; PREP: 15

Ingredients
- 3 bone in chicken breasts
- 1½ cups mayo
- 1 lemon juiced
- 3 tablespoons madras curry
- 2 stalks of celery, chopped
- 1 apple, peeled and diced
- ½ teaspoon black pepper
- salt and pepper
- ½ cup nuts, optional
- ¼ cups raisins or dried cherries, optional

1. Preheat oven to 350. Put the chicken breasts on a sheet pan and sprinkle with salt and pepper. Bake 40-50 minutes or until done.
2. Cool and then pull the meat from the bones and the skin off. Cut into bite size cubes and put into a bowl.
3. In a large bowl mix the dressing: add the mayo, lemon juice, curry powder and black pepper. Mix well and set aside.
4. Peel and core the apple, then dice into small chunks add to the bowl with the chicken.
5. Cut the celery in half length wise and then dice. Add to bowl with the chicken.
6. Add the nuts and dried fruit if desired to bowl also. Mix gently but make sure that all the ingredients are dispersed evenly.
7. Add the mix to the dressing and gently mix. Once mixed well refrigerate for at least an hour for the flavors to merge.
8. Serve on top of a mixed green salad.

GERMAN POTATO SALAD

This is my favorite potato salad. I am not a fan of the ones that add egg. I have had a lot of potato salads with a creamy sauce but the potatoes are bland. I like that this has clear strong flavors. The potatoes soak up the vinegar by adding them warm to the vinegar. The different mustards also add a lot of flavor. I created this recipe to have a bold taste. It is best if made a day ahead.

PREP TIME: 10 MINUTES; COOK TIME: 15 MINUTES; SERVES: 2

Ingredients

- ¼ cup mayonnaise
- 2 Tsp. whole grain mustard
- 1 Tbsp. red onion
- 1 Tbsp. cider vinegar
- fresh black pepper
- 2 Tsp. Dijon mustard
- 1 stalk of celery
- 1 tablespoon parsley
- 1 scallion (green onion)
- 5 red potatoes
- Optional: sliced red onions, sliced dill pickles, sliced gf salami

1. Place potatoes in a small sauce pot and cover with cold water. Bring up to a boil. Boil until tender 10-15 minutes. Use a fork to check for doneness. Drain. Rub the skins off the potatoes with a dishcloth.
2. Slice potatoes and place in a bowl with the vinegar. Toss well. Let cool on the counter. Stir occasionally to make sure the vinegar is soaked up.
3. Once the potatoes are cool. Chop the red onion, scallion and celery into small pieces. Add to the potatoes in the bowl.
4. Mix together mayonnaise, Dijon mustard, and whole grain mustard. Stir into the potato mixture. Add black pepper to taste. Chill.

GREEN PAPAYA SALAD

This is a refreshing salad to have next to some grilled meat or even as a stand alone dish. The health benefits of green papaya are incredible. This is one of my favorite crunch salads.

PREP 15; COOK: 0; SERVES 6

Ingredients

(salad, side dish)
- 2 green papayas
- 2 carrots
- 2 tbl minced mint leaves
- 1/3 cup cilantro leaves
- 2 large limes
- 2 Serrano chilies or thai bird chilies
- 2 tbl coconut sugar
- 3 tbl fish sauce
- 1 inch peeled fresh ginger
- 1 english cucumber

1. In a blender combine the lime juice, ginger, fish sauce, chiles and sugar and blend until smooth. Set aside.
2. Peel and seed papayas. Shred or use madeline an julienne the fruit. Put into large bowl. Julienne the cucumber after removing the seeds and add to the bowl.
3. Peel the carrots and julienne them. chop the mint leaves and half of the cilantro leaves and add to the bowl. Add the rest of the whole cilantro leaves. Toss gently and add the dressing toss again.
4. Garnish with chopped peanuts if desired.

GRILLED CESAR SALAD

Grilled Cesar salad is a fun take on the original salad. This recipe includes the recipe for vegan parmesan cheese that goes inside of the salad dressing.

Grilling the romaine lettuce adds a smokey taste to it and nice grill marks. This grilled Cesar salad is a perfect addition to a nice bbq dinner or as a meal with some grilled chicken slices added on top.

SERVES 3; PREP 10; COOK: 5-6 MINUTES

Ingredients
- 3 heads romaine hearts, sliced lengthwise in ½
- 3 garlic cloves
- 3 tablespoons fresh lemon juice
- 1 tablespoon dijon mustard
- ¾ cup good olive oil plus 3 tablespoons
- fresh black pepper
- For vegan Parmesan cheese
- ½ cup unsalted cashews
- 2 tablespoon brewer's or nutritional yeast
- ½ teaspoon fine sea salt

1. Pre heat grill to medium heat.
2. In a food processor put the cashews, nutritional yeast and salt. Blend until combined. Put in small bowl and set aside.
3. In blender combine the garlic, lemon juice, dijon mustard. With blender running, slowly pour the olive oil in so that it emulsifies (blends well).
4. Add the vegan parmesan cheese to the dressing and blend quickly.
5. Cut the lettuce hearts length wise and brush the lettuce with the olive oil. Sprinkle salt and pepper over the lettuce.
6. Grill for 2-3 minutes each side so that it gets grill marks on the lettuce and begins to wilt.
7. Place lettuce cut side up on a plate and drizzle with the Cesar dressing.
8. Add fresh black pepper if desired.

GRILLED CHICKEN ASIAN SALAD

This grilled Chicken asian salad is the star of my table on hot summer nights. I love big bold flavors. This crunchy salad full of veggies and herbs is tossed in a bold and almost spicy dressing that pared with tender chicken, toasted sesame seeds and toasted almonds will have you going for seconds or licking your bowl.

SERVES 4; PREP 10; COOK 20

Ingredients
- 4 boneless chicken breasts, grilled
- 1 napa cabbage, shredded
- 2 heads of romaine lettuce, shredded
- 2 carrots, grated
- 1 red bell pepper, thinly sliced
- ¼ cup slivered almonds, toasted
- 1 tablespoon toasted sesame seeds
- ¼ bunch of cilantro, chopped
- ¼ bunch mint, leaves chopped
- ½ cup bean sprouts
- ¼ cup olive oil
- 2 tablespoons tamari or gluten free soy sauce
- 2 tablespoons rice vinegar
- 3 teaspoons fresh grated ginger
- 1 teaspoon sesame oil
- 1 teaspoon sriricha sauce

1. In large jar, add the olive oil, tamari, rice vinegar, ginger, sesame oil and sriracha shake well to incorporate it well.
2. Shred the napa cabbage and romaine lettuce and put in a large bowl.
3. Shred the chicken breasts with two forks or cut into cubes. Add to the bowl.
4. Add the grated carrot, bell pepper, almonds, sesame seeds, bean sprouts, cilantro and mint to the bowl.
5. Add the salad dressing and toss the salad well.

LEMONY QUINOA TABOULI

This is one of my favorite salads! I love Tabouli, but I don't eat the bugler wheat it is normally made with any more, so I developed this recipe using quinoa. This recipe has all the flavor profile of the original plus extra lemon and it turns out delicious! I like a lot of flavor in my tabouli, so use the freshest ingredients you can for the best results.

SERVES 1; PREP 15; COOK 15

Ingredients
- 1/3 cup good organic virgin olive oil
- 1/3 cup fresh squeezed lemon juice
- 1 clove of garlic minced
- 1/2 cup packed mint leaves
- 1/2 teaspoon fresh ground black pepper
- 3/4 teaspoon salt
- 3 green onions
- 1 bunch parsley
- 3 large roma tomatoes or 4 small ones
- 1/2 english cucumber
- 1 cup uncooked quinoa

1. First make the dressing by combining the olive oil, lemon juice, garlic, mint, salt and pepper in a blender. Pour into a large mixing bowl and set aside.
2. Cook the quinoa according to package directions. It is usually 1 cup quinoa to 2 cups of water. Bring to a boil, cover and simmer 10-15 minutes. As soon it is done, immediately put the hot quinoa into the dressing and mix well. This way the quinoa will soak up all of the flavor. Set aside to cool.
3. Finely chop the parsley and the green onions and put into a bowl.
4. Cut the cucumber and take out the seeds. Chop and add to the bowl.
5. Seed the tomatoes and dice, add to the bowl.
6. Stir together gently. Add this mixture to the cooled quinoa mixture and toss gently. Cover and refrigerate for at least an hour so the flavors come together. I like to make this a day ahead.
7. I like to have this for a protein rich breakfast with some sliced fruit on the side. It makes a great meal or side dish for grilled chicken or fish.

LENTIL SALAD

Lentil salad gets made in my home quite often. It is easy to make, quite inexpensive and can be made so many different ways. In fact, lentils are high in protein and other essential nutrients including iron, potassium and many antioxidants. When you put them hot into a flavorful vinaigrette like in this recipe, they soak up the flavor.

I also love to make lentils and mix them with quinoa for a fun salad. They are great warm or cold. Delicious as a stand alone dish, a side dish or on top of a nice green salad.

SERVES: 4; PREP: 15; COOK: 20

Ingredients
- 1 cup dried lentils
- 4 cups of water
- ½ English cucumber, diced
- 2 roma tomatoes, seeded, diced
- ½ purple onion, diced
- 1 red pepper, diced
- 2 tablespoons fresh flat leaf parsley, chopped
- 3 tablespoons dijon mustard
- 3 tablespoons good olive oil
- ½ cup white balsamic vinegar (apple or white works also)
- ½ teaspoon salt
- fresh black pepper

1. In a medium saucepan bring the water and lentils up to boil. Cook over low heat until lentils just are tender. 15-25 minutes. Don't over cook or they turn into mush.
2. While the lentils are cooking, in a large bowl mix the olive oil, mustard, vinegar, salt and pepper with a fork or whisk until combined.
3. Prepare all the veggies and put in another bowl.
4. When the lentils are done, drain them with a strainer, getting all the water out.

Continued ➤

LENTIL SALAD *Continued*

5. Put the lentils into the mustard vinaigrette and gently, with a rubber spatula, incorporate the lentils into the dressing until they are coated. Let stand and get to room temp.
6. Once cooled, add the bowl of veggies and mix gently but mix well. Check for salt and pepper.
7. Chill the salad until ready to serve.

SEAWEED SALAD

Seaweed salad has been called "The Green Superfood' because it is full of antioxidants, calcium and vitamins. This version has tons of flavor because of the sesame oil, tamari, fresh ginger and garlic. It also has green onions, apple, cilantro and is topped with sesame seeds. This is the "Superfood" seaweed salad with a huge flavor punch!

I have had many varieties of seaweed salad but they all seemed to be missing something to make me want to eat it again or actually really enjoy it. When I added the thin stips of green apple to the salad, I got a nice variety of texture. The tamari, rice wine vinegar, sesame oil, ginger and garlic add to the great flavor. This is not your ordinary seaweed salad, you might just want to make double!

- ¾ ounce dried wake seaweed (whole or cut)
- 3 Tbsp rice vinegar
- 3 Tbsp tamari or coconut aminos
- 1 Tbsp sesame oil
- 1 Tsp finely grated fresh ginger
- 1 finely minced garlic clove
- 3 green onions finely sliced
- 1 small green apple cut into thin strips
- 2 Tbsp chopped fresh cilantro
- 1 Tbsp toasted sesame seeds
- ¼ tea red pepper flakes

1. Soak seaweed in warm water for 5 minutes. Drain, rinse and then squeeze out all excess water.
2. Cut into ½ inch strips.
3. In a bowl mix rice vinegar, tamari, sesame oil, ginger, garlic, onions, cilantro, sesame seeds and red pepper flakes together.
4. In another bowl mix the seaweed, apple and cilantro. Add the dressing and mix.

SPICY THAI STEAK SALAD

Summer hot weather has me cooking my proteins in the mornings and making a variety of cold salads for dinner. Fresh baby spinach, purple onions and juicy grilled flank steak make a fantastic summer dinner full of flavor and spice. Look for the Thai red chilies in your supermarket but if you cannot find them, feel free to substitute jalapeño chilies.

Ingredients

- 1-2 pound flank steak
- 2 fresh red chilies or jalapeños, sliced
- 3 cloves fresh garlic, minced
- 4 tablespoons fresh lime juice
- 1 purple onion, thinly sliced
- 4 green onions, cut into 1-inch slices
- 1 head of cilantro, roughly chopped, divided in half
- 3 tablespoons olive oil or melted coconut oil
- ½ teaspoon salt
- ¼ cup toasted sesame seeds, divided in half
- 4 cups Spinach greens

1. In a small bowl combine the chilies, garlic, fish sauce, lime juice, half the cilantro, green onions, oil and salt and mix well. Save 2 tablespoons of the marinade for dressing the salad.
2. Take the flank steak and make thin scores in it against the grain with the tip of a sharp knife.
3. Put the flank steak and the marinade into a large zip bag making sure the marinade gets all over the steak. Let it marinade in the fridge 2-4 hours.
4. Gill your steak until it is the desired doneness, about 8 minutes each side for medium rare and let it rest on a platter for 10 minutes.
5. In a large bowl, toss the spinach and sliced purple onion together with the reserved dressing.
6. Put salads on plate.
7. Cutting against the grain of the beef, make thin slices. Place slices on top of the salads and sprinkle the saved cilantro and sesame seeds over it.

SALAD

SUGAR SNAP PEA SALAD

I bought this huge bag of sugar snap peas at the farmers market because they were so delicious. I snacked on them as snacks for days and the bag never seemed to shrink. So I decided to turn them into a side dish to go with my chicken I was making for some friends who were coming over for dinner. My dinner's flavor profile was asian flavor so I whipped up this tasty side dish salad and loved it. It is great chilled in the summer, room temperature in the winter. It is one of my favorite go to side dishes!

SERVES 4; PREP 5 MINUTES; COOK 10 MINUTES

- 2 Cups sugar snap peas
- 1 Cup julienned cut carrots
- 3 Tbsp. sesame seeds
- ½ yellow onion, sliced thinly
- ½ Cup julienned red peppers
- 2 cloves garlic, minced
- 2 Tsp. sesame oil
- 3 Tsp. hoisin sauce
- 1 Tsp. ginger, grated
- 2 Tsp. gluten free soy sauce
- 1 Tbsp Coconut Oil
- 2-3 Tbsp. sesame seeds, toasted

1. Heat oil in small skillet over medium heat. Add onions, ginger and garlic. Cook for 2 minutes. Add soy sauce and hoisin sauce. Remove from burner and let cool.
2. Cook peas in salted boiling water for 2-3 minutes. Remove and rinse under cool water and drop into a bowl with ice water to shock them and keep them crisp and green.
3. Mix together the cooled peas with the sliced carrots, sliced onion and red bell pepper.
4. In a medium bowl, mix together the cooled sauce and the veggies. Toss well to coat and then sprinkle with sesame seeds.

SWEET POTATO SALAD WITH FRESH DILL

I wanted potato salad, but I no longer have potatoes in my food lifestyle except for sweet potatoes and yams. So I experimented by making a sweet potato salad and it turned out delicious! It has more flavor than the kind made with russet potatoes. I wish I had thought of this years ago!

The sweet potatoes in this salad not only add some sweetness and richness but they are packed full of vitamins and nutrients! This version is so much healthier than the old fashioned one by a long shot!

SERVES 4; PREP 10; COOK 5

Ingredients

- 2 sweet potatoes (medium sized)
- 4 stalks of celery
- 4 green onions
- 2 tablespoons fresh dill
- ¼ cup mayo
- ¼ cup coconut milk
- ½ teaspoon apple cider vinegar
- ⅛ teaspoon salt and ½ teaspoon salt
- ¼ teaspoon fresh ground black pepper

1. Peel and cut the sweet potatoes into small cubes. Put into a sauce pan of cold water with ½ teaspoon salt. Bring up to a boil and cook until fork tender, about 4-5 minutes.
2. While the potatoes are cooking make the sauce. In a bowl mix the mayo, coconut milk, apple cider vinegar, salt, pepper and fresh dill.
3. Dice the celery into small pieces and add to the bowl. Slice the green onions using both the green and white parts and add to the bowl.
4. When the potatoes are done, drain and add to the bowl with the sauce. Putting the potatoes warm in the sauce allows them to soak up all of the flavor.

TOMATO AVOCADO SALAD

I love fresh ripe tomatoes from the farmers market with avocados. It makes a perfect salad on a nice summers day.

SERVES 1; PREP 10;

Ingredients

- 1 ripe avocado
- 1 large ripe tomato
- 2 teaspoons fresh lemon juice
- 1 teaspoon red wine vinegar
- 3 teaspoons olive oil
- ½ teaspoon Dijon mustard
- 1-cup arugula
- Salt and pepper

1. Mix the fresh lemon juice, red wine vinegar, mustard and olive oil together in the bottom of a salad bowl.
2. Add salt and pepper to taste.
3. Cut avocado in half and remove seed.
4. Cut into quarters and peel.
5. Slice avocado into chunks.
6. Slice tomato into chunks.
7. Add avocado and tomato to dressing in bowl and mix.
8. Let stand 15 minutes to one hour.
9. Add arugula and toss well.

***Serving Suggestion:** Can substitute mixed greens for arugula. Add tuna to make salad an entrée.

Salad Dressings

Avocado Salad Dressing 140
Caesar Dressing 141
Garlic Lemon Sunflower Dressing 142
Honey Mustard Dressing 143
Mustard Balsamic Vinaigrette 144
Pear vinaigrette 145
Ranch Dressing 146

AVOCADO CAESAR DRESSING

Avocado is the secret to this delicious rich feeling version of caesar dressing. The capers and lemon juice are the magic ingredients that turn the humble avocado in to this glorious version of the dressing.

SERVES 4; PERP 10;

Ingredients
- 1 ripe avocado
- 3 Tbs lemon juice
- 2 Tbs water
- 1 clove minced garlic
- 1 Tbs capers
- 2 tsp dijon mustard
- ¼ tea Salt
- ¼ tea Pepper

1. Add all ingredients through Dijon mustard to blender and blend.
2. Add salt and pepper to taste.

CAESAR DRESSING

There are days that I want a crunchy delicious Cesar salad. This is a very easy dressing to make. Grinding up the capers and raw almonds are the magic trick to creating a fantastic dressing.

SERVINGS 8; PREP 5

Ingredients
- ½ cup raw sliced almonds
- 2 cloves chopped garlic
- 1 cup extra virgin olive oil
- juice of one lemon
- 4 tsp capers
- 1 cup mayonnaise
- ½ tsp pepper

Combine all ingredients in blender and mix well.

GARLIC LEMON SUNFLOWER DRESSING

I am always playing around with dressings in my kitchen. I have a lazy Susan that is filled with tons of flavored vinegars and flavored olive oils. I usually put a little dijon mustard in the bottom of my bowl, add the flavors I want of vinegar and oil and whisk that together.

Yet there are times I am craving a more hearty dressing that is a perfect match for some big leafy greens or to use over grilled chicken in lettuce leaves. This recipe is perfect for that. The base is sunflower seed butter which you can now find in most stores. If you cannot find it, you can substitute almond butter for it. It changes the taste a little but both versions are good.

PREP: 10; COOK: 0; SERVES: 4

Ingredients
- 3 tablespoons sunflower seed butter
- 2 tablespoons fresh lemon juice
- 2 tablespoons water
- 2 teaspoons pure maple syrup
- 2 cloves of garlic finely minced
- ¼ teaspoon cayenne pepper
- ¼ teaspoon fresh black pepper

Put all the ingredients into a blender and blend until well blended and smooth.

HONEY MUSTARD DRESSING

This makes a great dipping sauce for fresh veggie rolls in rice paper, as a salad dressing or a dip for chicken wings. It is super easy to use and it lasts for about a week in the fridge.

SERVES: 4; COOK: 0; PREP: 10

Ingredients

- ½ cup good mayo
- 2 tablespoons yellow mustard
- 1 tablespoon dijon mustard
- 3 tablespoons honey
- 2 tablespoons fresh squeezed lemon juice
- 1 teaspoon fresh tarragon, chopped
- 1 tablespoon good olive oil

Whisk all ingredients together. Store in jar with tight lid.

MUSTARD BALSAMIC VINAIGRETTE

I enjoy a fresh salad with a tasty salad dressing. I have found that easiest way to make the salad dressings is to make it in the bottom of the salad bowl before adding the greens. Making a fresh dressing only takes a few moments and is easy.

This mustard balsamic vinaigrette is one of my go to salad dressings as well as a marinade for grilled veggies and even flank steak. I have served it as a dip for fresh veggies and drizzled it over my chicken salad. The strong flavor adds a nice burst of flavor to any salad.

PREP: 5; COOK: 0; SERVES: 4

Ingredients
- ⅓ cup good virgin olive oil
- ¼ cup balsamic vinegar
- 1½ teaspoons dijon mustard
- ¼ teaspoon salt
- ¼ teaspoon fresh black pepper

1. Put all the ingredients in the bottom of a salad bowl and whisk until the dressing emulsifies. The mustard when whisked thickens and binds all the other ingredients.
2. Or put all the ingredients into a small jar and shake until emulsified.

PEAR VINAIGRETTE

This is a very easy salad dressing to make but it has a lot of flavor. By grilling the pear, you bring out the sweetness. If you do not have a grill you can broil the pear or even sauté it in a pan for a few minutes before blending.

PREP: 5; COOK 10; SERVES 4

Ingredients
- 1 ripe pear, cored
- ½ finely chopped onion
- ¼ cup red wine vinegar
- ½ cup good olive oil
- 1 teaspoon coconut oil
- 1 teaspoon dijon mustard

1. Core and peel pear. Cook on hot grill 3-5 minutes each side until the outside starts to caramelize.
2. Heat coconut oil in small frying pan and sautee onion until translucent about 5 minutes.
3. Place all ingredients into blender and blend. Taste for salt and pepper.

RANCH DRESSING

I wanted a dairy free ranch dressing to go with a Cobb salad I had made. I knew that traditional ranch dressing had dairy. My final version tastes so good and you would not know it has coconut milk in it because of all of the fresh dill, and it tastes like traditional ranch dressing! This dressing also works great as a dip for veggies.

SERVES 2 CUPS; PREP 15

Ingredients
- 1 cup mayo
- 1¼ cup coconut milk
- 3 tablespoons fresh chopped dill
- 3 cloves of garlic made into a paste with sea salt (use the flat side of your knife to do this)
- 1½ teaspoons apple cider vinegar
- ¾ teaspoon black pepper
- ⅛ teaspoon salt

Put all the ingredients into a blender and blend until smooth. (I actually put all the ingredients into a large glass jar and shake well.)

Seafood

Cilantro Grilled Shrimp 148
Fish en Papillote 149
Fish Taco Bowls 151
Garlic Shrimp 152
Halibut Kebabs 153
Halibut with Mango Salsa 154
Lemon Rosemary Salmon 155
Pecan Dill Crusted Salmon 156
Red Snapper Veracruz Style 157
Shrimp with Tomatoes and Olives 158
Tequila Orange prawns 159

CILANTRO GRILLED SHRIMP

Easy dish to make and goes great with a variety of dips. Or make a batch with saffron rice for a main meal.

SERVES 10; PREP: 10; COOK: 5 MIN

Ingredients
- ½ bunch cilantro, chopped
- 2 tablespoons olive oil
- 3 garlic cloves, minced
- 1 lime, juiced and zest
- ½ teaspoon salt
- 2 pounds uncooked medium shrimp, peeled and deveined

1. In a large resealable plastic bag, combine the cilantro, oil, lime juice, lime zest, salt and garlic. Add the shrimp; seal bag and turn to coat. Cover and refrigerate for 1 hour.
2. Thread shrimp onto skewers. Grill, covered, over medium heat for 2-3 minutes on each side or until shrimp start to turn pink and begin to shape the letter "c". Do not over cook, they will continue to cook once removed from heat.

FISH EN PAPILLOTE

I created this recipe because I wanted a flavorful fish dish for dinner but I did not feel like standing over a stove. By cooking the fish sealed up in parchment paper, the fish soaks up lots of flavor. The packet puffs up while it is cooking. When you cut it open, the aromatic steam escapes. This is an easy recipe and has a great wow factor. A delicious sauce is created with the liquid from the fish, the wine and lemon.

This recipe is for one but you could multiply it by as many as you desire, but make sure to wrap each serving individually in the parchment so everyone gets their own paper bowl. You can make these pockets ahead and keep in the fridge for a few hours until you are ready to bake. They are perfect for a dinner party.

SERVES 1; PEP 10; COOK 20

Ingredients
- 1 filet sole
- ½ cup bell peppers
- 2 slices fresh lemon
- 1 Tbsp. white wine
- ½ cup carrots
- 1 shallot sliced thin
- 1 Tsp. ginger
- salt and pepper
- ¼ teaspoon coconut oil melted

1. Take a piece of parchment paper and fold in half. Cut to resemble a large heart making sure that there is 2 inches of space around the filet. Cut the carrots and bell peppers into thin strips that resemble matchsticks. Slice the shallot and ginger very thin. Toss the carrots, bell pepper, shallot and ginger together. Place on one side of the heart.

2. Rinse off the fish and dry well. Place on top of the vegetables. Put the butter on the fish and season with salt and pepper. Top with the lemon slices.

Continued ➔

FISH EN PAPILLOTE *Continued*

3. Fold the other side of the heart over. Crimp the edges to seal starting at the fullest part of the heart and ending at the pointy end. Right before you finish sealing it, add the wine. Tuck the end under. You can also staple the edges once folded.
4. Place on baking sheet and cook in 400° oven. The parchment will be puffed up and browning when done. The fish will be flakey.
5. Serving Suggestions: Use yellow or red bell peppers for the best flavor. Substitute any mild white fish for the sole. Different herbs and vegetables change the entire dish. Make sure you use a good white wine that you would drink.

FISH TACO BOWLS

I love fish tacos and have been eating plenty of them as I am here at the beach in Mexico. I also like the ease of having everything in one dish. So I took the classic fish taco platter and put all the ingredients into one big bowl for ease.

PREP: 10; COOK: 10; SERVES: 4

Ingredients
- 4 fish filets (snapper, tilapia)
- 2 cups cooked brown rice
- 2 avocados diced
- 1 red onion
- 1 red bell pepper
- 1 can black beans rinsed
- ½ head fresh cilantro
- 2 tablespoons coconut oil
- 1 lime
- 2 teaspoons chili powder
- 3 teaspoons cumin
- ½ teaspoon salt
- ¼ teaspoon pepper

1. Sprinkle the chili powder, cumin, slat and pepper over all the sides of the fish filets.
2. In a large skillet, heat the coconut oil. Then add the fish filets making sure not to overlap. This step may be done in 2, by cooking 2 filets at a time if needed
3. Cook the fish 2-3 minutes each side, check for doneness in the center. Remove from heat when done and squeeze the juice of the lime over the fish filets.
4. Chop the cilantro and mix half into the brown rice and save half. Mix in the drained black beans into the rice mixture.
5. Put the brown rice in the bottom of each bowl.
6. In a bowl, mix the avocado, cilantro, onion and red bell pepper.
7. Put the fish on the rice in the bowl.
8. Put ¼ of the veggie mix over each filet .
9. Serve.

GARLIC SHRIMP

I love shrimp and garlic together. One day I realized it was after two in the afternoon and I had not eaten. I needed a quick tasty lunch. I always have frozen raw shrimp in the freezer. They defrost under running water in minutes. This is such a simple dish with simple clear flavors. I found that there are many ways to serve the shrimp once cooked. Some simple ways are over a spinach salad, with side dishes or tossed with noodles and olive oil. This is a perfect recipe for a quick healthy meal.

SERVES 4; PREP 10; COOK 5

Ingredients

- 24 large shrimp (21/25 count)
- 4-5 minced cloves of garlic minced
- 3 tablespoons coconut oil
- ¼ teaspoon red chili flakes

1. Peel and devein the shrimp. Rinse and dry well. Heat coconut oil in a large skillet over medium low heat. Add the garlic and pepper flakes. Cook for one minute. Add the shrimp.
2. Cook for 4 minutes or until done turning once. The shrimp will begin to turn orange and curl into a "C" shape when done. Do not overcook.
3. Serving Suggestions: Good over a spinach salad. Serve with rice and a vegetable. Chill and eat cold or put over a salad when cold. Can use more pepper flakes for more spice. Toss with gluten free pasta noodles and a little of the noodle water and olive oil to create a sauce.

SEAFOOD

HALIBUT KEBABS

Halibut kebabs are an easy and quick way to get dinner on the table! Halibut is a dense and firm fish that holds up well to being cubed, skewered and grilled. It has very little fat and requires little seasoning. This recipe combines olive oil, fresh rosemary and pancetta to create a mouth watering dish!

SERVES 4; PREP 5; COOK 6

Ingredients

- 1 - 1½ pounds fresh halibut, cut into chunks
- 3 ounces pancetta, thin sliced
- ¼ cup olive oil
- 1 tablespoon fresh lemon juice
- 1 tablespoon fresh rosemary, chopped
- 1 garlic clove, minced
- ½ teaspoon salt
- ¼ teaspoon black pepper

1. In a large bowl, add the olive oil, rosemary, garlic, lemon, clove, salt and pepper and mix well.
2. Take the skin off the halibut and cut into 2 inch chunks.
3. Add the halibut to the marinade mixture in the bowl and toss so that it coats all sides of the fish and let stand 5 minutes.
4. If you are using bamboo skewers soak them for 5 minutes in water.
5. Skewer the fish putting a thin slice of pancetta between each chunk. this should make 4 skewers full.
6. Over a medium high grill, grill the kebabs turning frequently taking care not to tear the fish.
7. Cook for 6 minutes or until the fish is cooked through.

HALIBUT WITH MANGO SALSA

This halibut with mango salsa is a quick, easy and delicious dish to make. One of my favorite things to eat is fish with a fresh mango salsa. It reminds me of having lunch on my Mother's porch in Mexico, feeling the soft breeze and watching the ocean waves. This recipe uses halibut but any other white fish will work. I also like to grill the fish and serve it with the salsa and warm corn tortillas as fish tacos. The salsa stays fresh in the refrigerator for three days.

SERVES: 4; PREP TIME: 15 MINUTES; COOK TIME: 10-15 MINUTES

Ingredients
- 4 Halibut filets
- 4 ripe mangos
- 3 large jalapeños
- 4 tablespoons olive oil
- 1½ tablespoons lime juice
- ½ red onion
- 4 tablespoons cilantro
- ½ teaspoon salt

1. Rinse fish under cold water and pat dry with paper towels.
2. Peel, seed and dice the mango and divide in half.
3. Seed, remove the membranes and dice the jalapeño and divide in half.
4. To make the marinade: combine half the mango, half the jalapeño, 1 tablespoon fresh lime juice, and 2 tablespoons olive oil. Mix well. Put fish in a plastic zip bag and pour marinade over. Turn fish in marinade so all of it is covered.
5. Make the salsa by combining the other half of the mango and jalapeño.
6. Add diced red onion, chopped cilantro, fresh lime juice and salt. Mix well. Set aside.
7. Remove fish from marinade. You can grill, broil or pan-sear the fish.
8. If you want to bake it, place in a small baking dish. Bake fish 400° for 15 minutes. Fish temperature should be 145°.
9. Serve with salsa on top of the fish.
10. Serving Suggestions: Serve with rice, beans and warm corn tortillas for fish tacos. Use any firm white fish with this salsa.

SEAFOOD

LEMON ROSEMARY SALMON

This is not your ordinary week day salmon recipe but it only takes moments to make. This salmon dish is packed full of unexpected flavor. The fun part is that each serving is cooked in its own package so presentation has a wow factor.

The flavors of the dijon mustard, white wine, lemon, capers and rosemary create a harmony of flavors for the mouth that have you coming back for more.

Prep the individual packages and then pop them in the oven right before you are ready to eat. Perfect dish for a dinner party also because you can make the packets ahead of time!

SERVES: 4; PREP: 15; COOK: 10

Ingredients

- 4 salmon filets
- 1 tablespoon finely minced fresh rosemary
- 2 lemons sliced thin
- 2 teaspoons dijon mustard
- 1 lemon juiced
- ½ cup good white wine
- 2 tablespoons capers
- ½ teaspoon salt
- ½ teaspoon black pepper
- 4 pieces of parchment or aluminum foil

1. Preheat oven to 400 degrees farinheight
2. Put four pieces of parchment or aluminum foil on the kitchen counter.
3. Place on file of salmon on each piece.
4. Sprinkle the fish with the salt and pepper. Then put ½ teaspoon of the mustard evenly over the top of the salmon.
5. Layer the thin slices of lemons over the top of the fish. Sprinkle each fish with some capers.
6. In a small bowl mix the wine and the lemon juice.
7. Pull up the sides of the foil to start to create packets for the fish. Pour the sauce evenly over each filet. Seal the packets well.
8. Place the packets on a baking dish and put into the oven. Bake 10 minutes.

PECAN DILL CRUSTED SALMON

This Pecan Dill Crusted Salmon is perfect for a dinner party or holiday meal. It is very easy to make and comes out of the oven looking so beautiful. The mixture of fresh dill, pecan nuts and garlic on top of the fish adds a lot of flavor and makes a great presentation.

SERVES 4; PREP 5; COOK 20

Ingredients

- ¾ cup pecan halves, roasted
- 2 garlic cloves, minced
- 4 tablespoons fresh dill, chopped2 tablespoons olive oil
- ½ teaspoon salt
- black pepper
- 4 salmon steaks

1. Pre heat oven to 400 degrees.
2. In a food processor, put in the pecan halves, garlic, dill, olive oil, salt and pepper. Process 4-6 times until it looks like bread crumbs.
3. Place the salmon on a baking sheet.
4. Put ¼ of the mix on the top of one fish steak, repeat on each steak.
5. Bake in oven 20 minutes until the fish is flakey.

RED SNAPPER VERACRUZ STYLE

As a child, I got to grow up in Mexico and Guatemala. My favorite thing to eat starting when I was 3 was a whole Huachinango fish (red snapper). I would eat it each day if my parents let me. To this day, it is my favorite fish and I still eat a whole pan-fried one on the beach when I go home to see my family. What a feast! This recipe is my version of a classic Mexican dish from Veracruz.

Veracruz borders the Gulf of Mexico. Veracruzano or Veracruz-style is distinct with its capers, green olives, olive oil, bay leaf and garlic. This recipe has a lot of flavor and is easy to make. This sauce is also quite delicious with shrimp.

SERVES 1; PREP 10; COOK 20

Ingredients
- 1 filet red snapper
- ½ jalapeño
- 1½ teaspoons olive oil
- ½ cup of chicken stock
- 1 Bay leaf
- 4 green pimento stuffed olives sliced
- 1 tomato
- 1 garlic clove
- 2 teaspoons of capers
- 1 tablespoon cilantro
- ⅛-¼ teaspoon salt

1. Seed and dice the tomato and the jalapeño. Slice the green olives and mince the garlic. Chop the cilantro.
2. In a small skillet, sauté the garlic, onion, and jalapeño with olive oil. Cook over medium low heat until onion is translucent and soft, about 3 minutes.
3. Add tomatoes, olives, bay leaf, capers, salt and chicken stock. Stir and cook for 5 minutes. Tomatoes will begin to break down and get soft.
4. Once the sauce has come together add the filet into the sauce. Spoon some of the sauce over the fish. Cook for 10 minutes, or until fish is done, turning once. Fish will flake apart easily.
5. Place fish on a plate and pour sauce over. Sprinkle with cilantro.
6. Serving Suggestions: Serve this with warm corn tortillas to soak up the sauce. The sauce can be made a day ahead and refrigerated.

SHRIMP WITH TOMATOES AND OLIVES

Italian Shrimp and Olives is a quick easy meal to make. I serve it over quinoa or brown rice, but it is good also over rice noodles. The olives add a touch of brine flavor to the sauce and the chili flakes just a little bit of heat. A super simple dish with a lot of flavor.

SERVES 4; PREP 10; COOK 20

Ingredients

- 1 pound shrimp, peel and devein (remove tails)
- 1 tablespoon coconut oil
- 1 yellow onion, diced fine
- 2 cloves garlic, minced
- 2 cans diced fire roasted tomatoes
- 1 cup pitted olives (green or black)
- ½ cup white wine
- 1 teaspoon salt
- ½ teaspoon pepper
- ½ teaspoon oregano
- ¼ teaspoon crushed red chili flakes

1. Over medium-high heat, heat up a large skillet with the coconut oil.
2. Add the onion and cook for 3-4 minutes until it starts to become translucent.
3. Add the garlic and cook for 1 minute more.
4. Add the tomatoes, olives, wine, salt, pepper, oregano and chili flakes to the pot.
5. Lower the heat to a simmer. Stirring occasionally cook 7-8 minutes.
6. Add the shrimp to the tomato mix. Cook 1-2 minutes on the first side until it begins to change colors.
7. Turn the shrimp over and cook 2-3 minutes until done. The shrimp will curl into a letter "C" as they are done and turn the stove off. They will continue to cook in the sauce since it is hot.
8. Serve immediately.
9. Serve over quinoa, brown rice or rice noodles.

TEQUILA ORANGE PRAWNS

This is a quick, easy and delicious meal. I like to make this recipe with large prawns but you can substitute shrimp for it, just use more. I love the flavor of the fresh orange with the tequila. The tequila add flavor to the marinade and cooks off quickly when the prawns are in the pan.I also like to leave the last segment of the tail and tail fin on the prawns for presentation and for easy eating if you want to forgo the knife and fork! I like to pare this prawn dish with my quinoa tabouli salad.

SERVES 1; PREP 5; COOK 3;

Ingredients
- 7 large prawns
- zest of one orange
- juice of one orange
- 3 Tablespoons good tequila
- 1 clove of garlic minced
- ¼ teaspoon salt
- few grinds of pepper
- 1 Tablespoon coconut oil

1. Prep the prawns by peeling them and leave the tail on. With a paring knife, slice down the back 2/3 of the way through so that it butterflies and can stand up. Remove the vein, rinse and pat dry.
2. In a large zip bag add the orange zest, orange juice, tequila, minced garlic, teaspoon and pepper. Mix well and add the shrimp. Zip closed and put in the fridge for ½ to 1 hour, shaking the bag on occasion to make sure the prawns soak up the flavor.
3. In a small frying pan heat the coconut oil. Once it is hot, place the prawns, butterflied side down curling the tail over it. Cook until it starts to turn pink, about 2 minutes. Sear each side quickly and the shrimp will turn orange and begin to curl into the letter C. Don't overcook.
4. Take out of the pan and plate. These are even good room temp or chilled the next day.

Side Dishes

Aloo gobi – Indian cauliflower and Potatoes 162
Bacon Kale Frittata..164
Cauliflower Fried Rice.. 165
Cauliflower with Lemon and Olives 166
Cilantro Spaghetti Squash............................. 167
Coconut Rice...168
Garlic Mashed Potatoes 169
Garlic Oven Asparagus..170
Garlic Spaghetti Squash 171
Green Beans and Mushrooms 172
Herb Garlic Brown Rice 173
Herb Sweet Potato Wedges............................ 174
Honey Glazed Carrots 175
Mushroom Risotto 176
Perfect Green Beans 177
Pesto Green Beans 178
Roasted Red Potatoes and Garlic................ 179
Sautéed Spinach 180
Steamed Zucchini.. 182
Stuffed Zucchini.. 183
Sweet Potato and Turnip Puree.................... 184

ALOO GOBI - INDIAN CAULIFLOWER AND POTATOES

I was singed up for Indian food cooking lessons and I had been to the local Indian spice store and purchased all the traditional spices. I even bought the traditional Indian spice box that is called Masala Dabba. It is a stainless steel round container with a lid and has 7 smaller round containers inside it and a special spoon. I had read 5 Indian cookbooks from cover to cover and I was ready.

The first dish we made was Aloo Gobi which is a traditional Indian cauliflower and potato dish. "Cauliflower is my first dish?" I thought. I wanted something super traditional and exciting. I was told this was a staple in most homes. I learned to make the ginger-garlic paste, the wet masala spice mix and I got to use the spiced in my new fancy Masala Dabba!

I was not ready for the most delicious mouth watering taste sensation that this seemingly simple dish had. "Oh my this is cauliflower and potatoes like I have never experienced them before!" The humble and often over looked cauliflower and potato was honored with all of the delicious spices. I have also had this dish where they put in green peas near the end.

I have adjusted the more labor intensive recipe to this recipe I use at home. It has all of the same flavor profiles but is much simpler to make.

PREP: 20; COOK: 30; SERVES: 4-6

Ingredients
- 1 small head of cauliflower, cut into small florets
- 3 potatoes, peeled and cut into ½ inch cubes
- 2 tablespoons coconut oil
- 1 teaspoon curry powder
- 1 teaspoon cumin
- ½ teaspoon turmeric
- 2 garlic cloves, minced
- ½ inch fresh ginger, grated
- ½ teaspoon salt
- 1 serrano pepper, cut in half lengthwise
- ¾ cup of water
- 4 tablespoons cilantro, rough chopped

SIDE DISHES

1. In a large pot over medium high heat, melt the coconut oil. Add the curry, cumin, turmeric, ginger, salt, garlic and serrano pepper. Stir and cook for 1 minute.
2. Add the cauliflower florets and diced potato to the pan along with the ¾ cup of the water. Stir well and get the seasonings all over every pice.
3. Cover and cook over medium high heat for 15 minutes. Remove the lid and stir.
4. Cook uncovered for 5-19 minutes until the cauliflower and potatoes are tender, stirring occasionally.
5. Garnish with chopped cilantro before serving.

BACON KALE FRITTATA

Frittatas are very easy to make and make a great breakfast, easy snack or even a light dinner. You can put most anything into a frittata. In this one I put bacon and kale which make a delicious combination.

SERVES 4; PREP 5; COOK 30

Ingredients

- 1 tablespoon coconut oil
- ½ yellow onion, chopped
- 4 slices bacon, chopped
- 2 cups kale, de-stemmed and chopped
- 8 large eggs
- ½ cup coconut milk (almond milk)
- ½ teaspoon salt
- black pepper

1. Pre heat oven to 350 degrees F.
2. In a large bowl beat the eggs well, add the coconut milk, salt and pepper and beat again.
3. In an oven proof skillet, heat the coconut oil over medium heat.
4. Add the bacon pieces to the pan and cook for 4 minutes.
5. Add the onion and cook 2 more minutes.
6. Add the kale to the pan and cook for 5 minutes.
7. Add the eggs to the pan, do not stir. Cook for 4 minutes over medium heat as the bottom and edges begin to set up.
8. Put the skillet in the oven and let cook 12-15 minutes or until the fritter is cooked all the way through.
9. Let it set on the counter 3-5 minutes before cutting.
10. This tastes good at room temperature also.

CAULIFLOWER FRIED RICE

When I first heard about cauliflower fried rice I was skeptical. The idea that cauliflower would taste as good as rice was in intriguing. So I made some. Wow! Then I tweaked it until I got it just right and that it is easy. This is not only a perfect side dish but late night meal or vegetarian entréee.

SERVES 4; PREP 15; COOK 20

Ingredients
- 1 head of cauliflower
- ½ lb (8 slices) of thick-sliced bacon
- 2 large eggs
- 1 Tbsp minced ginger
- 3 cloves of garlic, minced
- 2 carrots diced, about 1 cup
- ½ cup of peas, fresh or frozen
- 4 green onion, thinly sliced
- 2-3 Tbsp tamari
- 2 Tbsp coconut oil, divideded

1. Cut the cauliflower into florets, discarding the tough inner core. Working in batches, pulse the cauliflower in a food processor until it breaks down into rice-sized pieces.
2. Cook the bacon in a frying pan or in the oven until crispy Let cool and chop into small bits.
3. In a medium frying pan, heat 1 tablespoon of the coconut oil.
4. In a small bowl, scramble the 2 eggs and pour into the skillet. Cook and then chop into small bits.
5. In a medium frying pan, heat the other tablespoon of coconut oil. Add the carrots and cook for 2 minutes. Add the peas and cauliflower rice and mix ingredients well. Lower the heat to medium and cover. Cook until the cauliflower is done, about 7 minutes.
6. Uncover and stir in the bacon, eggs, green onions, and tamari and serve.

CAULIFLOWER WITH LEMON & OLIVES

I had a bunch of cauliflower from the famers market to cook up, but I wanted to do something new and different with it. I noticed that I have big fresh organic lemons and some local olives. Inspiration hit. Taking a vegetable that some see as boring into something exciting. Cauliflower is a perfect substitute for rice or even mashed potatoes, yet this recipe gives the vegetable the respect it deserves.

To really give it a zing of flavor I added some lovely shallots and fresh thyme. This truly touches all the savory areas of the tongue and gets them dancing. This is a perfect vegetarian meal or a great side dish to some lemon roasted chicken.

MAKES: 4 SERVINGS; PREP TIME: 25 MINUTES; COOK TIME: 7 MINUTES

Ingredients
- 1 large head cauliflower, trimmed and cut into bite-size pieces
- 2 lemons
- ¼ cup olives like kalmata olives
- 2 tablespoons good olive oil
- 2 shallots diced
- 1 teaspoon chopped fresh thyme
- ¼ teaspoon salt
- ¼ teaspoon freshly ground pepper

1. Put a steamer basket into a sauce pot that has a good lid. Add ¾ cup water (about 2 inches of water) to the pot. Take the trimmed cauliflower prices and put them in the steam basket, cover and bring to boil. Cook 5-7 minutes from the time you turned the pot on or until fork tender.
2. Zest the lemons.
3. Peel the lemons and with a sharp knife, cut the fruit segments out of the membranes and chop up the fruit.
4. Add the chopped lemon fruit, any juice that escaped and the zest to a large bowl.
5. Add the olive oil, minced shallots, chopped thyme, salt and pepper to the bowl. Stir well to combine.
6. Remove the cauliflower while still warm from the pan and toss in the lemon mixture.

CILANTRO SPAGHETTI SQUASH

This cilantro spaghetti squash is something I serve with my garlic shrimp recipe often. It takes the place of the shrimp scampi and pasta that I use to make all the time. Not only is the shrimp dish delightful and flavorful, you will be surprised how great the combo of cilantro and spaghetti squash is!

SERVES 4; PREP 10; COOK 50

Ingredients

- 1 spaghetti squash, halved lengthwise and seeded
- 2 tablespoons extra-virgin olive oil
- ½ teaspoon salt
- ½ bunch chopped fresh cilantro
- ¼ teaspoon fresh ground pepper

1. Pre heat the oven to 400 degrees F
2. Cut the squash in half and scoop out the seeds.
3. Poke holes in the skin side of the squash and place cut side down on a baking sheet.
4. Bake 50 minutes and remove when the skin begins to turn brown.
5. Chop the Cilantro and toss in a bowl with the olive oil, salt and pepper.
6. Taking a fork, scrape the squash out in strands and add to the bowl. Toss well.
7. Add extra cilantro as a garnish if desired.

COCONUT RICE

I was working on my first cookbook a few years ago and the teenager I was raising asked me to make a sweet rice dish. I was not a fan of rice pudding and wanted to come up with something different. I had just finished my Thai Cooking Classes with Chef Chat Mingkwan in Sonoma, California and was enjoying that flavor profile. I swapped out the water for coconut milk, toasted up some unsweetened coconut flakes I had on hand and created sweet mouthfuls of flavor!

I actually had forgotten about this recipe until the teenager, now a grown up and a Chef for a fantastic Restaurant in Napa, California mentioned it. He had come for his mail and asked me for the recipe. I had to dig through a file of very messy, food stained sheets of paper to find it. That night I made it again to make sure it was as my memory had me thinking it was. The dish turned out fantastic and I pared it with some spicy chicken tikka masala, what a great combination! The left over rice is also a great one to turn into a veggie fried rice for an unexpected flavor profile.

PREP: 5: COOK: 20; SERVES: 6

Ingredients
- 2 cups Jasmine rice
- 1½ cups water
- 1 can unsweetened coconut milk
- 1 teaspoon salt
- 1½ cups unsweetened coconut shreds

1. In a medium sauce pan add the water, coconut milk and salt, stir.
2. Add the rice and stir again.
3. Bring rice up to boil, cover and let simmer 20 minutes. Do not lift the lid during the cooking process.
4. When the rice is done, do not uncover, turn off heat and let stand 10 minutes.
5. In a large skillet sprinkle in the coconut shreds. Toast them stirring occasionally until they turn light brown. Take off heat and let cool.
6. Stir the toasted coconut into the rice and serve.

SIDE DISHES

GARLIC MASHED POTATOES

These garlic mashed potatoes are so very good you will never miss the butter. By simmering the garlic cloves slowly with the potato chunks and then mashing together, it allows the garlic flavor to penetrate the potatoes in a very good way.

SERVES 8-10; PREP 15; COOK 25

Ingredients
- 6 russet potatoes, peeled and cut into equal size chunks
- 1 whole head of garlic, all cloves peeled
- 1 teaspoon salt
- ½ teaspoon fresh black pepper
- ½ - ¾ cup good chicken stock

1. In a large soup pot, cover the potatoes with cold water.
2. Add the garlic cloves and bring up to a boil.
3. Lower heat to simmer. (This slow cooking of potatoes will infuse them with the garlic flavor.)
4. Simmer until potatoes are fork tender about 20-25 minutes.
5. Drain the potatoes and garlic cloves.
6. Put the garlic cloves and potatoes back in hot pot.
7. Add stock, salt and pepper and mash.
8. Add more stock if needed.

GARLIC OVEN ASPARAGUS

This is one of my favorite easy side dishes that come out amazing. I use to always marinate my asparagus this way and then grill them for the smoking flavor. Yet the oven version is even easier and always comes out great. I cook mine until they are soft but still have a little crunch in the middle.

PREP: 10; COOK: 10-15 MIN; SERVES: 6

Ingredients

- 2 pounds fresh asparagus, ends removed
- 4 cloves of garlic minced finely
- 1½ tablespoons melted coconut oil
- ½ teaspoon salt
- ¼ -½ teaspoon fresh black pepper

1. Preheat oven to 450
2. Remove the woody ends off of the asparagus and place in a large zip baggie.
3. Finely mince the garlic and add to the asparagus in the bag.
4. Add the melted coconut oil, salt and black pepper
5. Remove the excess air out of the bag and then gently massage the asparagus in the bag so the coconut oil, garlic, salt and pepper are evenly distributed with the asparagus.
6. Let sit for 30 min to marinate. (This can be done a day ahead.)
7. Cover your baking sheet with parchment paper.
8. Arrange your asparagus on the sheet making sure not to overlap.
9. Place sheet in oven and bake 10-15 depending on the thickness of the asparagus and the texture you desire.
10. Remove and plate. Taste for salt and pepper, if you need more add it.

GARLIC SPAGHETTI SQUASH

This garlic spaghetti squash has become one of my favorite dishes since it tastes so decadent. After the squash is roasted and the strands are pulled apart with a fork, it is gently heated in oil that has been infused with fresh garlic, salt and pepper. This gently coats the strands of squash with delicious flavor.

PREP 5; COOK 1 HOUR; SERVES 4

Ingredients
- 1 large spaghetti squash
- 3 cloves finely minced garlic
- 3 tbl olive oil (or coconut oil)
- ¼-½ tea salt
- ¼ tea black pepper

1. Cut the squash in half. Scoop out the seeds and place face down on a baking sheet. Poke holes in the back with a fork.
2. Bake in a preheated 400 degree oven for 50 minutes and when they start to turn brown. Pull out and let sit on counter until cool.
3. While the squash is cooling, heat the oil in a small frying pan over low heat with the salt, pepper and finely minced garlic. Stir occasionally and do not let burn. Cook about 10 min on low.
4. Using a fork, scrape out the spaghetti like strands of the squash onto the sheet tray. Pulling them apart so they are not clumps.
5. Add the squash to the oil mix stirring to mix well. Heat through. Serve warm as a side dish.

GREEN BEANS AND MUSHROOMS

This is a very easy, tasty side dish to toss together and put into the oven. I get rave reviews every time I do it. I think because it is roasted and not many people think of roasting green beans. The magic trick in this side dish is the thin sliced garlic. Now you might be tempted to just chop it but don't. The thin slices are pretty and add such great flavor. The balsamic vinegar adds the right tang to the whole dish.

SERVES 4; PREP 10; COOK 30

Ingredients
- 2 Cups thin green beans
- 3 cloves garlic
- 1 Tbsp. extra virgin olive oil
- 2 Cups mushrooms
- 3 Tbsp. balsamic vinegar
- ½ Tsp. salt
- Fresh ground black pepper

1. Wash and cut the ends off the green beans and cut into 1 inch pieces. Slice mushrooms into thick slices. Peel garlic and cut into thin slices. Put chopped ingredients in large bowl with vinegar, extra virgin olive oil, salt and pepper. Mix well.

2. Pour into an ovenproof baking dish. Bake for 30 minutes uncovered, stirring once during baking. Beans will still have some crispness and mushrooms will be soft and garlic will taste sweet.

3. Serving Suggestions: This dish is also good at room temperature. I prefer baby bella mushrooms but you can use any type of mushrooms.

HERB GARLIC BROWN RICE

I love brown rice and having rice as a side dish, but I also like creating unexpected flavors in my rice that wake up your taste buds. This garlic herb rice dish does just that.

The garlic is sautéed and then gently cooked in the rice with stock to add tons of flavor. The unique and flavorful herb mixture is added at the end so that the flavor is fresh.

This rice dish is a perfect side to a fish or chicken dish any night of the week. It has a wow factor that will impress guests, while only taking you minutes in the kitchen.

PREP: 15; COOK:50; SERVES: 4; med skill

Ingredients

- 1 cup brown rice
- 2 cups stock (chicken or vegetable)
- juice of one lemon
- zest of one lemon
- 1 teaspoon coconut oil
- 10-12 garlic cloves finely minced
- 2 tablespoons finely chopped rosemary
- 2 tablespoons finely chopped mint
- ¼ cup finely chopped Italian parsley
- ¼ cup finely chopped cilantro

1. In a medium sauce pan over medium heat, heat the coconut oil. Then add the minced garlic cloves and stir well. Cook for about 1-2 minutes until it starts to change color. Add the rice and stir well. Cook for 2 minutes.
2. Add the broth to the rice and bring up to boil. Cover, reduce heat to low and cook for 50 minutes. Do not take off lid during cooking process.
3. When the rice is done immediately stir in the lemon juice and zest quickly. Let set 5 minutes.
4. Then pour the rice into a bowl and gently stir in all the fresh herbs. Serve while warm.

HERB SWEET POTATO WEDGES

I fell in love with sweet potato fries the second I tried them. I have had them thin, thick, spicy, garlicky, sweet... I was convinced since they were made from sweet potatoes (which we know are better than russet potatoes) that they were healthy fries. Wrong. Most of the time they are fried in hydrogenated oil which has trans fats and those are the worst type of fat you can consume.

Hence the GSDF makeover of the classic sweet potato fries. This is my grown up version with fresh herbs. The trick is they are not fried, they are baked. Yet they are baked at a high temperature so they have the right crunch. I use coconut oil, which is a very healthy oil and works very well at high temperatures.

If you want to turn these into garlic herb fries, sauté the garlic stovetop and pour over the fries when they get plated so that the garlic does not burn.

PREP: 15; COOK: 20; SERVES: 4-6

Ingredients
- 6 medium sweet potatoes
- 3 tablespoons coconut oil melted
- 1 teaspoon salt
- ½ teaspoon ground pepper
- 3 teaspoons fresh thyme leaves
- ½ teaspoon dried basil
- ⅛ teaspoon cayenne chili powder

1. Preheat oven to 500°.
2. Peel the sweet potatoes. Then cut lengthwise into half, then 3-4 wedges per half lengthwise depending on thickness desired. You will get 6 or 8 wedges depending.
3. Place potatoes in a large bowl; coat with coconut oil, tossing well.
4. Combine salt, pepper, thyme, basil and cayenne in a small bowl, mixing well.
5. Sprinkle the herb mixture over potatoes, tossing well to coat.
6. Arrange potatoes, cut sides down, in a single layer on a baking sheet.
7. Bake for 10 minutes; turn wedges over.
8. Bake an additional 10 minutes or until tender and beginning to brown.

SIDE DISHES

HONEY GLAZED CARROTS

Simple good quality ingredients do not need a lot of help in the kitchen. I brought home beautiful rainbow carrots from the farmers market and they were so sweet.

Cooking the carrots until they are just fork tender and then glazing them in the wonderful honey mix makes them the star of the dinner plate.

Don't under estimate the delicious carrots as a nice side dish.

PREP 5; COOK 15; SERVES 4

Ingredients
- 1 pound baby carrots (or carrots cut into 1 inch pieces)
- 3 tablespoons raw honey
- 1 tablespoon coconut oil
- ¾ teaspoon salt, divided
- 1 tablespoon lemon juice
- 2 tablespoons chopped Italian parsley
- ¼ teaspoon fresh black pepper
- 2 cups of water

1. In medium sauce pan put the two cups of water in and bring up to boil over medium high heat. Add ½ teaspoon salt.
2. When the water is boiling add the carrots. Cook until tender over medium heat. 6-8 minutes. Check to make sure they are fork tender. Then Drain.
3. In the saucepan add the coconut oil, raw honey, lemon juice, ¼ teaspoon salt and black pepper. Cook over medium heat.
4. Once the honey is warmed up add the carrots and cook for about 5 minutes, stirring well. Add the parsley and serve.

MUSHROOM RISOTTO

My favorite type of risotto is with mushrooms. This recipe turns out very creamy, rich and delicious. This recipe is earthy from the mushrooms and comforting. This is definitely another family favorite!

SERVES: 4; PREP TIME: 10 MINUTES; COOK TIME: 50 MINUTES

Ingredients

- 2 cup sArborio rice
- 8 cups chicken broth
- ½ cup white wine
- 1 yellow onion minced
- 3 cloves of garlic minced
- 2 tablespoons coconut oil
- 1 teaspoon salt
- 1 teaspoon fresh black pepper
- 12 ounces shiitake mushrooms sliced

1. Place the chicken stock in a pan on the stove and keep warm.
2. Sauté chopped onion in the coconut oil for 3 minutes. Add the minced garlic and cook for 2 minutes longer. Add the sliced mushrooms and stir well, coating the slices in the butter olive oil mixture. Cook 5 minutes. Add the rice to toast and stir well. Cook for 3 minutes.
3. Add the wine to the rice mixture and cook for 4 minutes. Add the warm chicken broth ½ cup at a time. Stir well. Add the salt and pepper. Let the rice soak up the broth before adding another ½ cup full. Do this until the rice is done, and tender to bite, about 30 minutes. You may have some stock left over.

PERFECT GREEN BEANS

This simple but delicious side dish will make any meal a special occasion. It is very easy to do but turns out great. You can even blanch the beans the day before you want to serve them and that way it will only take moments to finish the dish and bring it to the table hot.

PREP 10; COOK 5; SERVES 4-6

Ingredients
- 1 pound of French green beans (haricots verts)
- 2 cloves of garlic sliced thin
- ¼ teaspoon salt
- ¼ teaspoon black pepper
- 1 tablespoon coconut oil

1. Put a large pot of water to boil on the stove. Drop the green beans into the water for 2 minutes.
2. Drain the beans and immediately put into ice water to cool quickly and then onto a kitchen towel to dry.
3. In a large frying pan heat up the coconut oil over medium heat.
4. Add the thin sliced garlic and cook for 2-3 minutes.
5. Add the green beans and toss with the coconut oil and garlic. Sprinkle the salt and pepper over the beans and toss to mix well.
6. Cook for another 2 minutes until the beans are tender but still a little crispy.

NOTE: One of my favorite salts to use in this dish is grey mineral black truffle salt.

PESTO GREEN BEANS

Pesto green beans made with a fresh vegan almond pesto is a great side dish for some grilled chicken or fish. The crispy green beans soak up the delicious pesto and add flavor to your dinner plate. Feel free to use more garlic or red pepper flakes if you want it to have more garlic flavor and spice. These pesto green beans are great room temperature or the next day chilled from the fridge. Feel free to add some halved cheery tomatoes or sautéed mushroom slices to the dish also.

SERVES 4-6; PREP 15; COOK 3-5

Ingredients
- 2 pounds green beans
- 1 cup almonds, toasted and cooled
- ⅓ cup vegan parmesan cheese
- 1 cup Italian Parsley, chopped
- 1 small garlic clove, minced
- ½ teaspoons fresh thyme leaves, chopped
- ¼ teaspoon red pepper flakes
- ½ teaspoon salt
- ⅓ cup good olive oil
- Vegan Parmesan Cheese
- ½ cup unsalted cashews
- 2 tablespoon brewer's or nutritional yeast
- ½ teaspoon fine sea salt

1. Wash and trim your green beans.
2. Bring a large pot of salted water to boil.
3. Blanch the beans. This means to drop them into the boiling water for 3 minutes. Drain. Then plunge them into a large bowl of ice water. This keeps them crisp and their color.
4. Dry the beans.
5. In a food processor put the cashews, nutritional yeast and salt. Blend until combined. Put in small bowl and set aside.
6. In a food processor going the almonds, vegan cheese, garlic, thyme, red pepper, parsley and salt. Add the olive oil and process again.
7. Toss cooled green beans with the pesto.

SIDE DISHES

ROASTED RED POTATOES AND GARLIC

I first learned to make this dish when I was learning to cook at the age of 22. I was following a recipe that I got in a cookbook as a gift. The book had pictures I remember. That recipe had a chicken breast cooking on top of the potatoes it looked pretty fancy. This is my version of that recipe. It is one of my favorite side dishes and is very easy. I serve it when I roast chicken or grill a steak. I like how the outside of the potato gets crispy and the inside is creamy.

SERVES 4; PREP 5; COOK 45

Ingredients
- 3 cups small red potatoes
- 3 Tbsp. olive oil
- 12-15 cloves of garlic smashed
- 1 Tbl fresh rosemary
- ¼ Tsp. pepper
- 1 Tsp. salt

1. Pre heat oven to 400 degrees F.
2. Cut potatoes into 1-inch wedges. Chop the rosemary. Toss the potatoes with olive oil, garlic cloves, rosemary, salt and pepper. Place in baking dish, skin side up.
3. Bake 400° for 35 minutes.
4. Turn potato pieces over being careful not to tear the crispy crust that has formed on the potatoes. Bake 10 more minutes.
5. Serving Suggestions: Garlic cloves may be left whole. For variety use red, yellow and purple small potatoes. Add Diced onion to the mixture before baking. Dried rosemary may be substituted, use ¼ teaspoon.

SAUTÉED SPINACH

I took myself to dinner to a steak house when I was out of town on business. I ordered a steak and a side of sautéed spinach. I could not get enough of the sautéed spinach because it was the best I have ever had. The waiter asked the chef for the recipe but he would not give it up. The chef did send me two more side dishes of spinach on the house since I made such a big deal about it. I ate it all and took my steak home!

I have been on a mission to recreate this spinach dish. I have tried all kinds of ways. I did it and even better! Now I am addicted to this dish! In fact I just ran to the grocery to pick up another 2 bunches of spinach!

Remember that when cooking spinach it really shrinks down, so you will need more than you think you do. Always wash your spinach. The water in my sink is always so dirty after I was spinach. There is always some dirt mixed in with the leaves.

Serves 2-3; Prep 15; Cook 5

Ingredients

- 1 bunch of fresh spinach, washed, dried and the stalks pulled off (no need to chop)
- 1 tablespoon coconut oil
- 2 cloves of garlic
- ¼ teaspoon salt
- Fresh ground black pepper
- 1 tablespon rice vinegar

1. Chop the cloves of garlic very fine. Then sprinkle with a little sea salt. Using the back of your knife (the flat side) press and scrape across your cutting board the garlic. Do this until the cloves make a paste.
2. Heat the oil with the garlic and the black pepper. I like flavoring the oil before the spinach goes in because that way the spinach picks up all the flavor.

SIDE DISHES

3. Once the oil is hot, add your spinach leaves. Toss with tongs making sure all the leaves get some of the flavored oil. Near the end, when they are almost all totally wilted, add the vinegar. You usually have 15-30 seconds left of cooking at this point because spinach cooks so fast.
4. This dash of vinegar is what makes this dish come alive!
5. You can also add a chopped clove of garlic to the olive oil mixture if you want chunks of garlic also. The paste is important because it then coats all of the leaves.

STEAMED ZUCCHINI

Steamed zucchini can seem like a boring side dish, but I have a trick that has my dinner guests gobbling it up. In fact most don't even know I do it they just really like my steamed zucchini. I love the power of fresh herbs. When you steam herbs and squash together, the vegetable gets infused with the flavor of the herb.

PREP: 10; COOK: 3-5 MIN; SERVES: 4

Ingredients

- 4 medium sized zucchini, cut into one inch rounds
- ½ bunch fresh thyme
- ¼ teaspoon salt
- fresh black pepper

1. In a sauce pot put 2 inches of water and a steamer basket in the bottom.
2. Line the steamer basket with the little branches of thyme.
3. Lay the rings of zucchini on top of the thyme and cover.
4. Over medium high heat let the water come to a boil and the squash steam until fork tender. Do not over cook!
5. Remove the zucchini onto a serving platter and sprinkle with salt and pepper.
6. Garnish with fresh thyme if desired.

STUFFED ZUCCHINI

I love to make these zucchini boats as either a main dish or as a fun veggie side dish. They can be made ahead of time and baked in the oven right before you eat. You can mix up the veggies used in this to make it your own.

SERVES: 4; PREP:15; COOK:30

Ingredients
- 4 medium zucchinis
- 1 cup mushrooms, minced
- 1 bell pepper, diced small
- 2 cloves garlic, minced
- 1 yellow onion, diced
- 2 roma tomatoes, seeded and diced
- 1 teaspoon oregano
- 1 teaspoon salt
- 1 teaspoon basil
- 2 tablespoons coconut oil

1. Preheat oven to 350
2. Cut the ends off of the zucchini. Then cut in half length wise. Using a spoon, scoop out the seeds.
3. In a large skillet heat the oil.
4. Dice and mince the veggies and put into the skillet over medium heat.
5. Add the seasonings and stir, continuing to cook until veggies are cooked. About 5 minutes.
6. Let the veggies cool.
7. Stuff the zucchini boats and place on parchment on a baking sheet.
8. Bake in oven for 25 or until zucchini is tender.
9. Variation: Add vegan mozzarella cheese to the top of the boats the last 5 minutes.
10. Variation: Add gluten free bread crumbs to some melted coconut oil and sprinkle over the top before baking.

SWEET POTATO AND TURNIP PUREE

The sweetness of the lovely sweet potatoes blended with the spicy notes of the turnip turn an ordinary side dish into something quite extraordinary. It was an experiment because I had a 20 pound bag of sweet potatoes and was getting tired of either roasting them or mashing them. So I added turnips to the mix. It was so good the first batch got eaten as we stood in the kitchen trying it. The second batch was shared with friends who could not seem to get enough of this mix. Easy to do with fabulous results!

SERVES 4; PREP: 15; COOK: 15

Ingredients
- 3 sweet potatoes
- 1 turnip
- ½ cup chicken or vegetable stock
- ½ tea salt
- black pepper

1. Peel the sweet potatoes and turnip. Dice into large pieces and place in a pan filled with cold water. Heat the pan over medium high heat. Cook until fork tender about 10 minutes.
2. Drain potatoes and turnip, put into blender with the stock, salt and pepper and puree.

Soups

Asparagus Herb Soup 186
Beef and Quinoa Soup 187
Carne Asada Bean Soup 188
Celery Root and Apple Soup 190
Chicken tortilla Soup 191
Easy Broccoli Soup 193
Fennel and Kale Soup with White Beans 194
Fire Roasted Tomato Soup 195
Greek Wedding Soup 196
Hearty Vegetable Soup 197
Lentil Soup 198
Potato Leek Soup 199
Pumpkin and Carrot Soup 200
Roasted Eggplant Soup 201
Spicy Parsnip Soup 202
Thai chicken Coconut Soup (Tom Kha Gai) . 203

ASPARAGUS HERB SOUP

I adore asparagus in almost every form except out of a can. On this particular rainy spring day, I was craving soup but my fridge was full of spring veggies, hence the creation of this soup. While making this soup, I added peas for sweetness. This is a perfect soup warm but is actually quite delicious cold also.

Serves 4; Prep 10; Cook 15

Ingredients
- 1 pound asparagus
- 1 cup English peas
- ½ yellow onion minced
- 2 cloves garlic, minced
- 4 cups organic chicken stock
- ½ tsp. Salt
- ½ teaspoon pepper
- 1 tablespoon fresh chopped parsley
- 1 tablespoon chives divided
- ½ tsp. fresh lemon juice
- 1 tablespoon coconut oil

1. Cut woody ends off asparagus and toss. Cut tops off and reserve. Cut remaining asparagus into small pieces, about a ½ inch long.
2. In a small sauce pan, over medium heat, heat the coconut oil and sauté the minced onion until it's translucent, about 3 minutes. Add minced garlic and cook for 1 minute, making sure it does not brown.
3. Add peas, chicken stock, salt and pepper to the onions and garlic. Cook 3 minutes. Add chopped asparagus. Cook until tender, 3-5 minutes.
4. Puree soup with an immersion blender or blender using caution because hot liquid expands in the blender.
5. If using blender, return to pot over medium heat. Add lemon juice and asparagus tips, stir.

BEEF AND QUINOA SOUP

This is my GSDF version of what I use to make which was Beef and Barley Soup. I actually prefer this version. I found that when using quinoa I like to make the beef cubed a little smaller than I did in the original version.

Serves 6; Prep 15; Cook 90

Ingredients
- 1 lb Sirloin or Ribeye Steak, trimmed excess fat, cubed (about ½ inch pieces)
- 1 Tbsp Olive Oil
- 1 Large Yellow Onion, diced
- 4 Cloves Garlic, minced
- 2 Carrots, peeled and diced
- 3 Ribs Celery, diced
- 2 Medium Potatoes, diced
- 1 Bay Leaf
- ½ Cup Quinoa
- 6 to 7 Cups of Beef Stock
- 1 teaspoon Salt
- ½ teaspoon Black Pepper

1. In a large skillet add the olive oil over medium heat.
2. Once it is hot add the brown beef and cook browning all the sides, about 5-6 minutes.
3. Remove from pan and set aside.
4. In the same skillet add the onion and garlic.
5. Cook until onion is translucent being careful to stir and not burn the garlic.
6. Add the carrots, celery and potatoes to the mix. Stir.
7. Cook for 10 minutes until vegetables begin to soften.
8. Transfer the mix to a soup pot over medium heat.
9. Add the meat, stock, quinoa, salt and pepper.
10. Bring up to a bubble, cover and simmer for 1½ hours. Stirring occasionally.

OR

11. Transfer everything to a slow cooker and cook on low for 3-4 hours.

CARNE ASADA BEAN SOUP

This Carne Asada Bean soup is a full meal in a bowl! I will teach you a trick that will blow your mind. I found this trick a few years ago. Beans usually need to be soaked before cooking. No soaking using this fool proof method!

Serves 4-6; prep 10; cook 2 ½ hours

Ingredients
- 1 pound of beans
- 4 cups chicken stock
- ½ an onion
- 3 cloves of garlic
- 1 Tbsp. cumin
- 1 Tbsp. chili powder
- Tbsp. Garlic Powder
- 1 lbs. carne asada meat or thin sliced round sirlion
- One can of fire roasted tomatoes
- One can of green chilies
- One diced onion
- Salt
- *Optional Tbsp. fresh chopped cilantro and 1 lime to taste

1. Pre-heat oven 300 Degrees
2. Put 1 pound of been in a dutch oven and cover with chicken stock until it is about 3 inches higher than the beans
3. Add ½ an onion, whole and 3 cloves of garlic, 1 Tbsp. cumin and 1 Tbsp. chili powder (NO salt)
4. Bring to a boil
5. Cover with tight lid and put into oven for 75 minutes
6. Take your meat and season with salt, pepper, chili power and garlic powder
7. Cook then chop into bit size pieces
8. Remove the beans from the oven add the cooked meat
9. Add one can of fire roasted tomatoes
10. Add one can of green chilies
11. Add one diced onion

SOUPS

12. Add some more chicken stock
13. Add some salt now.
14. Simmer on stove for about an 45 minutes to an hour
    Remove from heat and serve

*serve with fresh chopped cilantro or lime if desired

**Note: I added more garlic when I added the diced onion and more chili powder and cumin to taste

**Note: I added more garlic when I added the diced onion and more chili powder and cumin to taste

CELERY ROOT AND APPLE SOUP

My first experience with celery root was in cooking school in Paris, France. I had never seen it and had no idea what to do with that funny bumpy root veggie.

In cooking school we had gone to the farmers market to purchase the ingredients for that days lesson. Celery root salad was what we made. We peeled and diced the root, cooked it and made it into a delicious salad with lentils that was topped with chunks of gorgonzola cheese.

In the years since I have discovered how versatile a vegetable celery root is. It is great mashed as a side dish. But cooked with apples, onion and topped with bacon, celery root makes a marvelous soup.

PREP 20; COOK 30; FEEDS 4

Ingredients
- 1 large celery root
- 2 large granny smith apples
- 1 yellow onion
- 4 cups chicken stock (or veggie stock)
- ¼ cup coconut oil
- 2 pieces of bacon
- ½ tea salt
- ¼ tea pepper

1. Peel and dice the celery root. Peel, core and dice the apples. Chop the onion.
2. In a soup pan melt the coconut oil and then add the celery root, apples and onion. Cook for 15 minutes, stirring occasionally until they are translucent.
3. Add the broth, salt and pepper and bring to simmer. Cover and reduce the heat to low. Cook 30 minutes stirring occasionally.
4. While the soup is cooking put the bacon on a baking sheet into a 400 degree oven. Bake until crispy 10-15 minutes. Keeping an eye on it. Drain on paper towels and then crumble into a bowl. Set aside.
5. Blend the soup in blender or with immersion blender taking care because it is very hot.
6. Pour the soup into bowls and sprinkle the bacon over the top.

SOUPS

CHICKEN TORTILLA SOUP

I love a good spicy chicken tortilla soup. This version is not spicy but has a lot of flavor so that the whole family can enjoy it. This is one of my go to soups when I have a cold or on a cold winters day.

The vibrant flavors and fresh veggies along with the avocado make this soup a one bowl meal.

It is easy to prepare and will cook on the stove with out a lot of work. Roasting bone in chicken breasts add a lot of flavor to both the chicken its self as well as the soup.

SERVES 8; PREP 10; COOK 90 MINUTES

Ingredients

- 2 bone in chicken breasts, roasted
- 1 can fire roasted tomatoes
- 1 diced yellow onion
- 3 cloves garlic, minced
- ½ bell pepper, diced
- 1 can green chilies
- 3 tbl tomato paste
- 8 cups chicken stock
- 6 corn tortillas
- 1 tea chili powder
- 2 tea cumin
- ½ tea salt
- 1 tbl coconut oil
- 2 avocados
- ½ diced red onion
- 1 bunch cilantro, chopped
- 2 limes quartered

1. Preheat oven to 350 degrees.
2. Place chicken breast skin up on a baking sheet. Season with a pinch of salt and cumin. Bake for 50 minutes. Set aside to cool.
3. Chop the onions, cilantro, garlic and bell pepper.
4. Heat the coconut oil in a large soup pot
5. Add the yellow onion, bell pepper and garlic.
6. Sauté until the onion is translucent about 5 minutes.

Continued ➜

CHICKEN TORTILLA SOUP *Continued*

7. Add the cumin, chili powder and salt. Stir well
8. Then add the stock, green chilies and roasted tomatoes.
9. Using two forks shred the chicken meat and take off the bone.
10. Add to the soup.
11. Add the tomato paste and stir well.
12. Bring up to boil then lower to simmer and cook for 90 minutes uncovered.
13. While the soup is cooking, cut the corn tortillas into 2 inch strips.
14. Put on baking sheet and back into a 400 degree oven. Bake until crisp about 5- 7 minutes. (You can also add the tortillas to the soup not toasted. Just add to the soup itself in the last 10 minutes of cooking so that they get super soft.)
15. Serve the soup in large bowls and top with the tortilla strips, avocado, red onion, cilantro and a squeeze of lime.

EASY BROCCOLI SOUP

A few winters ago, I was hungry, cold and wanted soup. I did not want to go out into the wind and rain. So I looked to see what I had on hand that I could make soup out of. I had a ton of fresh broccoli on hand. So I made a large pot of soup from the broccoli. I added a little onion and garlic hoping it would work. I loved the flavor of the soup. I poured it hot into my mug and would drink it as I worked on my computer. It has a comforting feel to it. This is currently my go to soup!

SERVES: 2; PREP TIME: 5 MINUTES; COOK TIME: 25 MINUTES

Ingredients
- 4 cups broccoli florets
- ½ yellow onion
- 1 clove of garlic
- 4 cups of chicken stock
- 1 tablespoon olive oil
- salt and pepper to taste
- ½ cup coconut milk (optional)

1. Slice the onion and garlic. In the soup pan, sauté the onion and garlic in olive oil. Cook until translucent. Add the broccoli florets and cover with chicken stock. Put the lid on and cook until tender, 25 minutes.

2. Uncover and turn off. Either use an immersion blender and blend, or use a blender. If using a blender, do in small batches because hot liquids expand. Add salt and pepper to taste.

3. coconut milk to soup and heat on medium low. This soup freezes well.

FENNEL AND KALE SOUP WITH WHITE BEANS

The fennel is such a nice addition to this kale and white bean soup. This is an easy soup to make with a lot of flavor that is good enough to serve to company. I made it one day when I was cleaning out the fridge and my plan was to use up the veggies in a soup. I had forgotten that I had picked up fennel at the local farmers market so I added it to the soup along with some ground fennel seeds to boost the flavor. The fresh lemon juice at the end allows the flavors to explode.

SERVES 6; PREP 15; COOK 45

Ingredients

- 2 Tbs coconut oil
- 1½ cup onions
- 2 cloves garlic
- 2 tsp salt
- 2 tsp ground fennel seeds
- 2 cup diced fennel
- 1 cup diced carrots
- 1½ cup diced potatoes
- 2 tsp thyme
- ¼ tsp black pepper
- 1-15 oz can fire roasted tomatoes
- 3 cups cooked white beans
- 4 cups vegetable or chicken stock
- 5 cups kale
- juice of one lemon

1. Dice the onion, mince the garlic and chop the kale.
2. Dice the fennel, carrots and potatoes in evenly sized small pieces.
3. In large soup pot, heat the oil over medium heat.
4. Sauté the onions, garlic, salt, fennel, carrots and potatoes until veggies are fork tender.
5. Add the fire roasted tomatoes, stock, ground fennel seeds, thyme and black pepper to the veggies. Stir to combine.
6. Bring to a simmer and cover. Cook for 30 minutes.
7. Add the drained beans and chopped kale to the soup and stir. Simmer for another 15 minutes.
8. Mix in lemon juice just before serving.

FIRE ROASTED TOMATO SOUP

This is a super easy delicious soup to make that not only is GSDF but because there is a potato blended in the soup, has the same qualities as cream of tomato soup. The soup is a perfect satisfying meal on its own or great with a nice salad. I love adding things to my tomato soup: popcorn, lump crab meat, fresh grilled prawns, diced brown cubes of potatoes that are nice and crisp. The tomato soup is a perfect canvas for a culinary imagination.

SERVES: 4-6; PREP 15; COOK 30

Ingredients
- 2 cans of fire roasted tomatoes
- 1 medium potato, peeled and diced
- 1 carrot, diced
- ½ yellow onion, diced
- 2 cloves of garlic, minced
- 1½ cups of vegetable stock
- ½ teaspoon salt
- ¼ teaspoon fresh black pepper
- 1 tablespoon coconut oil

1. Place soup pot on stove over medium heat. Add the coconut oil to the pot and let it melt.
2. Add the onion, carrot and garlic to the pot and cook for 10 minutes, stirring so that the garlic does not brown and the veggies get nice and tender.
3. Add all the rest of the ingredients, bring up to boil, lower the heat to simmer and cook 20 minutes.
4. Blend the soup. Either use an immersion blender or a blender. If using a blender, do it in small batches.
5. Once it is blended taste for salt and pepper, add more if needed.

GREEK WEDDING SOUP

This soup usually has orzo in it but that is gluten. You can add the miracle orzo noodles made out of plants. Instead what I did was added some chopped kale for nutrition and for texture which I think makes a nice addition to the classic soup.

SERVES: 4; COOK: 15; PREP: 15

Ingredients

- 8 cups chicken stock
- ¾ pounds ground lamb, beef or lamb/beef mix
- ½ cup Italian parsley, chopped
- ½ cup mint leaves, chopped
- 3 sprigs oregano, chopped
- 3 cloves garlic, finely minced
- 1 egg, beaten
- ⅓ cup gluten free bread crumbs
- ½ teaspoon salt
- fresh black pepper
- 1 lemon, zested and juiced
- 2 cups kale, chopped

1. In a large dutch oven heat up the chicken stock to a boil and then lower to a simmer. Add the kale.
2. In a large bowl add the meat, egg, gluten free bread crumbs, oregano, half the sparsely, half the mint, salt and pepper.
3. Using your fingers mix well but do not over mix.
4. Form into 1-inch balls and put into the stock.
5. Let cook 10 minutes.
6. Add the lemon juice, zest and the rest of the fresh herbs.
7. Cook 5 minutes more.

HEARTY VEGETABLE SOUP

This past winter was rainy and I love how the house smells when soup is cooking on the stove. Aromas of garlic, onion and fresh vegetables drift through the house. I decided that Saturdays would be vegetable soup night. I would clean out the refrigerator of all produce because Sunday mornings are the farmers market. This is a rustic soup with big chunks of vegetables and flavor. Don't let the list of ingredients spook you, it is a very easy soup to make and you can use what vegetables you have on hand.

SERVES 6; PREP 10; COOK 30

Ingredients

- 1 Tbsp. olive oil
- 2 cloves garlic chopped
- ¼ cup good white wine
- 1-cup broccoli florets
- 2 small carrots peeled and diced
- ½ teaspoon dried oregano
- ½ can fire roasted tomatoes chopped
- ½ onion chopped
- 6 crimini (baby bella) mushrooms sliced
- 1 large handful baby spinach
- 1 cup green beans cut into one inch pieces
- 1 small zucchini diced
- 2 cups chicken or vegetable stock
- 3 small red potatoes diced
- fresh ground black pepper
- ½ to 1 teaspoon salt
- optional: ½ teaspoon herbs de provence

1. Sauté onions and garlic in olive oil, in a small pot, over medium heat, until translucent.
2. Add mushrooms and white wine.
3. Cook for 5 minutes over medium low heat so that the mushrooms can absorb most of the liquid and flavor.
4. Add rest of the ingredients including the liquid and seasonings all at once. Bring up to a bubble, lower the heat and partially cover for 20 minutes.

LENTIL SOUP

This is an easy to make hearty soup. I love lentils and they come in many colors. I think I used green ones when I wrote this recipe. In doing some research, I even found heirloom brands of lentils. This is a pretty classic recipe with carrots, onions, celery and fire roasted tomatoes. It is one of my go to recipes that always turns out delicious.

SERVES 6; PREP 15; COOK 45

Ingredients

- 2 cups dried lentils (green or red)
- 32 ounce box of vegetable or chicken broth
- 4 carrots peeled and diced
- 2 celery stalks diced
- 1 yellow onion diced
- 3 cloves of garlic minced
- 1 can fire roasted tomatoes
- 2 tablespoons tomato paste
- 1 tablespoon coconut oil
- 1 teaspoon dried thyme
- ½ teaspoon dried oregano
- ½ teaspoon cumin
- 1 teaspoon salt
- fresh black pepper

1. In a soup pot heat the coconut oil over medium heat. Add the onions, garlic, carrots and celery. Cook until onions are translucent about 6-7 minutes.
2. Add the lentils, tomatoes, broth and all the seasonings. Stir to combine. Bring up to bubble and then lower a heat to simmer and cover. Cook 35-40 minutes until the lentils are tender.

OR

3. After the vegetables have cooked, place them and all the rest of the ingredients into a slow cooker and cook low 8-10 hours or on high for 4-5 hours.

POTATO LEEK SOUP

I will admit that I love soup in the winter. A bowl of it makes a great lunch or a coffee mug full makes a great snack. This soup is so creamy, hearty and tasty. I was craving soup and baked potatoes and this is what I made. It is easy to make and very filling.

PREP TIME: 5 MINUTES; COOK TIME: 30 MINUTES; SERVES: 2

Ingredients
- 1 leek sliced
- 1 russet potato
- 1 tablespoon coconut oil
- 1 clove garlic
- 3 cups of chicken stock
- ½ teaspoon salt
- ¼ teaspoon pepper

Slice leek and rinse in a bowl of water to remove any sand. Remove leek and dry on a dishtowel. Peel and dice the potato. Mince the clove of garlic.

Sauté the leek in butter over medium low heat. Cook for 5 minutes. Leek will get soft and start to fall apart. Add garlic and cook 3 minutes.

Add potato, stock, salt and pepper to the leek and garlic, stir. Bring to a boil and then simmer for 20 minutes. Blend soup in a blender or with an emersion blender until smooth. Serve hot.

PUMPKIN CARROT SOUP

Sweet pumpkin and carrot soup is a favorite. This is not the soup made from the giant orange pumpkins that get carved or from the kind pumpkin pie is made from. This soup is made from those small sweet pumpkins. With a bit of cumin, turmeric and cinnamon, it comes alive in your mouth. It is a comfort soup and is also great the next day.

SERVES 6; PREP 10; COOK 60

Ingredients
- small pumpkin (Baby Bear, Sugar Pie or Cheese Pumpkin)
- 1 pound of carrots
- 6 cups vegetable stock
- 1 yellow onion, dice
- 3 cloves garlic, mince finely
- 1 teaspoon cumin
- 1 teaspoon turmeric
- ½ teaspoon cinnamon
- ½ teaspoon dry mustard
- 3 tablespoons coconut oil, divided
- ¾ -1 teaspoon salt
- ½ ground black pepper

1. Preheat oven to 400 F
2. Peel the pumpkin, take out the seeds and set aside, cut flesh of pumpkin into ½ inch pieces.
3. Peel the carrots and cut into half inch pieces.
4. Place the pumpkin, carrots and 2 tablespoons of olive oil in a bowl and toss so that every thing gets coated evenly. Pour onto a baking sheet, spreading out the pieces. Roast for 30 minutes.
5. Place a soup pot on the stove over medium heat. Add the 1 tablespoon of coconut oil and the onion. Cook stirring for 10 minutes until translucent.
6. Add garlic, cumin, turmeric, cinnamon, dry mustard, salt, pepper, the roasted pumpkin, carrots and stir to coat with the seasonings. Add the stock and stir. Bring up to bubble, reduce heat to simmer and cover. Cook for 30 minutes.
7. Puree the soup. Use an immersion blender or a blender being careful not to burn your self or splatter the hot soup.
8. Check to see if it needs more salt or pepper.
9. Serve with toasted seeds if desired.

ROASTED EGGPLANT SOUP

As I was writing my cookbook, I was thinking of different soups to make. I happened to have an eggplant on hand. So I decided to make soup out of it. The soup turned out really delicious. I made two versions. The first version tastes like creamy roasted garlic and eggplant. The second version, using tahini (sesame paste), cumin and cashew cream add an exotic flavor that is earthy and creamy.

SERVES 2; PREP 10; COOK 40

Ingredients
- 1 medium eggplant
- 2 small tomato
- 2 tablespoons olive oil
- ¼ teaspoon pepper
- 1 small yellow onion
- 4 cups of chicken stock
- ¼ and ½ teaspoon salt
- 6 whole cloves of garlic in their skin

1. Cut eggplant in half.
2. Peel and cut onion in half and cut the tomatoes in half.
3. Place all items plus the whole garlic cloves on cookie sheet and toss with olive oil and ¼ teaspoon salt.
4. Bake in 400° oven for 20 minutes. The eggplant will be soft and begin to brown.
5. Scoop pulp out of eggplant discarding the skin and place in soup pot.
6. Squeeze the garlic pulp out of the skin and add to the eggplant.
7. Add tomatoes, onion and chicken stock.
8. Puree soup in blender in small batches or use an immersion blender.
9. Season with salt and pepper to taste.
10. Cook over medium low heat 20 minutes.

SPICY PARSNIP SOUP

Parsnips are often over looked and they are a great root veggie. Roasted they are so sweet and sautéed a little spicy. Don't underestimate these white over grown looking carrots, they are much more than how they appear. Pared with onion, ginger, good stock and a chili, they make one of the most delicious soups ever! This is perfect for a chilly fall or winter day. If you want it really spicy don't take the seeds out of the chili.

Ingredients
- 2 tablespoons coconut oil
- 1 yellow onion, chopped
- 2 cloves garlic, minced
- 1 thumb-sized piece fresh ginger , peeled and roughly chopped
- 1 tablespoon garam masala
- 6 parsnips , peeled and chopped into chunks
- 1 can unsweetened coconut milk
- 4 cups organic vegetable stock
- ½ teaspoon salt
- freshly ground black pepper
- 1 fresh red chili , deseeded and finely sliced
- 1 handful fresh cilantro, chopped

In a soup pot, heat up the coconut oil over medium heat.

Add the onion, garlic, ginger and garam masala.

Gently cook over medium low heat for around 10 minutes, until the onions are soft and sweet. Stirring occasionally.

Add the chopped parsnip and stir well.

Add the coconut milk, stock, salt, pepper and the chili.

Simmer for 30 minutes with a lid on, until parsnips are fork tender.

Carefully remove them from the heat.

Using a hand blender or blender, blend the soup.

Serve with some of the cilantro.

THAI CHICKEN COCONUT SOUP (TOM KHA GAI)

I love Thai food so much that I decided years ago to learn how to make it. I got to study with well known Chef Chat Mingkwan in Sonoma California. I learned so much from him about Thai cooking. The hardest part about preparing the meal is all of the prep work. So many steps go into creating the curry pastes, the broths, the dressings, the marinades and more.

My goal is to take those traditional Thai flavor profiles and make it easy for the home cook to recreate the dish. Tom Kha Gai, Thai chicken coconut soup is one of my go to soups when I want to make something quick, spicy and delicious.

The soup traditionally calls for kaffir lime leaves which add the unique lime flavor but in this version we will use lime. I also use ginger instead of galangal. Yet if you can find these items locally, use the traditional ones!

This recipe calls for lemongrass but if you can not find it, substitute zest of a lemon and ½ teaspoon grated ginger.

PREP: 15; COOK: 20; SERVES: 4-6

Ingredients

- 2 inch piece of ginger, sliced into thin rings
- 4 cups good chicken stock
- 1 can unsweetened coconut milk
- 1 lime, zested
- ¼ cup fresh lime juice
- 2 tablespoons fish sauce (3 crabs brand)
- 1 tablespoon coconut sugar
- 2 thai red chilis or jalapeño chiles, cut length wise
- 1½ cups thinly sliced cooked chicken
- 8 ounces shiitake, oyster, baby bella mushrooms, thinly sliced
- 2 lemongrass stalks, smashed with knife and then cut into 2" pieces
- ¼ cup fresh cilantro chopped for garnish
- chili oil optional

Continued ➔

THAI CHICKEN COCONUT SOUP (TOM KHA GAI) *Continued*

1. In a large soup pan, put the broth, lemongrass, chilies and ginger into the pan. Bring up to boil, reduce heat and simmer for 10 minutes. Then strain the soup taking out the solids.
2. Add the cooked chicken and mushrooms to the stock and cook over medium heat for 10 minutes.
3. Add the coconut milk, fish sauce and sugar. cook for 10 more minutes. Serve and garnish with cilantro.
4. Sprinkle some chili oil over the top of the soup if you want more spice.

Sweet Treats

Avocado Chocolate Mousse 206
Banana Pancakes 207
Chocolate Chia Seed Pudding 208
Cinnamon Baked Apples 209
Overnight Banana Chocolate Oatmeal 210
Pumpkin Bars 211
Quick Coconut and Chia Seed Pudding 213
Wine Poached Pears 214

AVOCADO CHOCOLATE MOUSSE

One of my favorite desserts after a good meal use to be chocolate mousse. When I went dairy free, I thought the days of having a decadent chocolate thick and rich mousse were over. They were not! In fact, I prefer this avocado mousse to the traditional dairy one. Just note, it will not taste like avocado at all. Use good cacao powder when making this. Once it sets in the fridge, it will be a great sweet chocolate end to a great meal!

SERVES 2; PREP 10;

Ingredients
- 1 ripe avocado
- ⅓ cup cacao powder
- ¼ cup honey
- ¼ cup almond or coconut milk
- 1-2 tsp vanilla extract

1. Blend all ingredients in blender, scraping down sides until thoroughly mixed.
2. Chill in refrigerator for 2-3 hours.

BANANA PANCAKES

These banana pancakes are super easy and delicious.

SERVES 2; PREP 5; COOK 5

Ingredients
- 1 Large Banana
- 2 eggs
- 1 Tsp coconut oil
- ¼ Tsp vanilla extract
- ¼ Tsp salt

1. Peel the banana and put it into a large bowl.
2. Mash the banana really well with a potato masher or fork until it is really smooth.
3. In a second bowl beat the eggs well. Add the eggs to the banana mixture along with the vanilla and salt. Mix well.
4. Or Put the peeled banana, eggs, vanilla and salt in blender and blend well.
5. In a small skillet heat the coconut oil.
6. Once the oil is heated add half of the batter. Cook like you would a normal pancake, flipping it half way through.

CHOCOLATE CHIA SEED PUDDING

Yes you can have your dessert and know that it will tame your chocolate craving but it also is packed full of nutrients with very few calories. One ounce has 11 grams of fiber, 4 grams of protein and lots of other vitamins and nutrients. This recipe allows for the creamy chia seeds to expand in the coconut milk to create smooth spoonfuls of goodness. Add the dark cocoa powder and a drizzle of heaven, and yes it is quite divine and delicious. So, yes, you can have chocolate dessert for breakfast if you wish!

SERVES 2; PREP 5

Ingredients

- 1 can organic coconut milk
- 1 tsp pure vanilla extract
- ¼ tsp sea salt
- ¼-cup chia seeds
- ¼-cup shredded unsweetened coconut
- 2-2 ½ tablespoons unsweetened cocoa powder
- 2 teaspoons honey
- ½-cup fresh raspberries or mixed berries

1. In a bowl add coconut, chia seeds, coconut milk, vanilla, honey, cocoa powder and salt
2. Mix until very well combined.
3. Place in the refrigerator and allow to chill for at least 2 hours
4. Serve with fresh raspberries, mixed berries or a fruit of your choice.

CINNAMON BAKED APPLES

I love the variety of apples in the fall especially this season. A new farmers market store opened up near me and they only carry what the local farmers grow. There were so many varieties of apples that I never knew existed until this year! I would grab 3 every time I found a new variety. Somehow along the way of tasting every variety this store carried, I had an apple problem. I started craving them. I would eat the whole apple core and all, slice them up and snack on them and then...

....I started baking them. Delicious organic sweet apples stuffed with a little coconut oil, lots of cinnamon and some cardamom and I was in heaven. This recipe is for whole cooked apples but works with peeled sliced apples also. It smells divine as it cooks and it is a delicious treat that has no guilt.

SERVES 4; PREP 15; COOK 60

Ingredients
- 4 whole organic apples of your choice
- 4 tablespoons coconut oil
- 1 tablespoon cinnamon
- 1 tablespoon cardamom
- ¼ teaspoon salt

1. Preheat oven to 350 degrees F
2. Cut the cores out of the apples leaving the bottoms intact. Place in baking dish.
3. In a bowl mix the coconut oil, salt, cinnamon and cardamom together well.
4. Fill each hole in the apple with 1 tablespoon of the mix.
5. Bake uncovered 50-60 minutes until soft and tender.

OVERNIGHT BANANA CHOCOLATE OATMEAL

Lets admit that sometimes we don't have time to make breakfast but we really want something divine and healthy to eat. This is a great recipe to do. You put it together, put it in the fridge overnight and in the morning you have a scrumptious feast!

PREP: 10 MIN; COOK: NONE; SERVES: 1

- 1 ripe banana, chopped
- 1 tablespoon raw cacao poder
- 1 cup unsweetened vanilla almond milk
- ¾ gluten free organic oats
- 1 tablespoon chia seeds
- ½ tablespoon maple syrup
- 1 tablespoon almonds or pecans, optional for topping

1. In a small mason jar, mix all ingredients except the banana until well combined.
2. Cover with a lid and refrigerate overnight (about 8 hours).
3. In the morning, mix in one chopped banana and sprinkle with nuts.

SWEET TREATS

PUMPKIN BARS

The crust on these pumpkin bars are made with walnuts and dates which adds a great texture to these delightful pumpkin bars. Move over pumpkin pie, there is a new GSDF Pumpkin Bar in town and we can't keep them around enough!

SERVES 16; PREP 15; COOK 50

Ingredients

For The Crust:
- 1 2/3 cups walnuts, toasted
- 1 cup pitted dates
- 4 tablespoons maple syrup or use stevia drops 1/4 teaspoon vanilla extract
- 2/3 cup rolled oats
- 1/2 teaspoon salt
- 1 teaspoon cinnamon
- 1/4 teaspoon nutmeg

For the Filling:
- 1 can of pumpkin (15 ounce)
- 1 can organic unsweetened coconut milk 1/4 cup stevia drops
- 1/4 cup raisins
- 2 eggs
- 2 tsp cinnamon
- 1 tsp ground ginger
- 1/2 tsp ground nutmeg
- 1/4 tsp ground allspice
- 1/2 tsp salt

For the Crust:
1. Preheat oven to 350 degrees F
2. In a food processor, process the walnuts, dates, maple syrup, and vanilla until the walnuts and dates are well broken down and you have a sticky mixture.
3. Add the rolled oats and pulse un- til they are incorporated.
4. Press the mixture into a 13 x 9 inch baking dish using your fingers to get it firm and even.

Continued ➜

PUMPKIN BARS *Continued*

For the Filling:
1. In a medium bowl, mix together the pumpkin, coconut milk, stevia, raisins, eggs, cinnamon, ground ginger, nutmeg, allspice and salt.
2. Mix very well.
3. Pour the mixture over the crust.
4. Bake uncovered until the filling is set 45-50 minutes. Cool and then cut into bars.

QUICK COCONUT CHIA SEED PUDDING

I discovered that chia seeds were really good for me. So at first I started sprinkling them on my daily oatmeal. I loved the crunch in the oats. Then I started thinking that a dessert would be a good idea. I looked in the pantry and found coconut milk and the rest is history. Chia pudding was discovered and devoured.

SERVING 2; PREP 5

- 1 can organic coconut milk
- 1 tsp pure vanilla extract
- ¼ tsp sea salt
- ¼-cup chia seeds
- ¼-cup shredded unsweetened coconut
- ½-cup fresh raspberries or mixed berries

1. In a pitcher add coconut, chia seeds, coconut milk, vanilla and salt
2. Mix until very well combined.
3. Place in the refrigerator and allow to chill for at least 2 hours
4. Serve with fresh raspberries, mixed berries or a fruit of your choice.

WINE POACHED PEARS

These wine poached pears make a great fall dessert. This recipe uses red wine but a nice port or sweet white wine also make fantastic poached pears. Top with a little cashew cream that has a touch of lemon zest if desired.

SERVES 6; PREP 5; COOK 25

Ingredients

- 3 large firm pears
- 2 cups nice red wine
- ½ cup of water
- 2 cinnamon sticks
- 2 star anise
- ¼ teaspoon salt

1. Peel and core the pears and then cut in half lengthwise.
2. In a medium saucepan, add the wine, water, cinnamon sticks, star anise and salt. Over medium low bring up to a simmer.
3. Add the pears to the poaching liquid face down, cover the pot and simmer 10 minutes.
4. Turn the pears over, cover the pot and simmer for another 15 minutes.
5. To serve: Plate the pear halves with the inside portion up and spoon some of the cooking liquid over.
6. Top with cashew cream and lemon zest if desired.

Vegetarian

Baked Portobello Mushrooms 216
Curry Sweet Potato Wedges 217
Fall Vegetable Curry.. 218
Grilled Artichoke with Lemon Aioli 219
Hemp Seed Pesto 220
Layered Ratatouille 221
Lemon Cauliflower... 223
Lentils and Rice (Mujadrah)..........................224
Moroccan Inspired Veggie Chickpea Soup... 225
Quinoa Enchilada Bake 226
Quinoa Root Veggie Stuffed Cabbage 227
Shepherd's Pie 229
Spicy Indian Dal (lentils) 230
Stuffed Eggplant 232
Stuffed Poblano Pepper................................. 233
Sweet Potato Enchiladas 235
Thai Inspired Almond Nut Sauce.................236
Vegan Alfredo Sauce....................................... 237
Vegetarian Chili.. 238
Warm Herb Olives... 239

BAKED PORTOBELLO MUSHROOM

Over twenty years ago, I met one of my best friends at work. She was a vegetarian. At the time I was a huge meat eater and only had vegetables as a side dish not as an entrée. We went out to dinner one night and she ordered this stuffed Portobello mushroom that was delicious. As I was creating my first cookbook, and was focusing on the vegetarian section, I thought of what she might like to eat. This is my version of the stuffed Portobello mushroom she ordered so many years ago.

SERVES: 2; PREP TIME: 10 MINUTES; COOK TIME: 30 MINUTES

Ingredients

- 2 Portobello mushroom cleaned
- 2 garlic cloves minced
- 2 roma tomatoes seeded and diced
- 1 small zucchini finely chopped
- 2 tablespoon parsley chopped, divided
- 4 tablespoons gluten free bread crumbs, divided
- ½ yellow onion finely diced
- salt and pepper
- 2 tablespoons, 2 teaspoons coconut oil divided

1. Cut the stem out of the mushroom caps and dice. Set aside.
2. Using a spoon scoop the gills out of the underside of the cap gently not breaking the mushroom cap.
3. Turn cap over, rub 1 tablespoon of coconut oil on the top of the mushroom cap. Sprinkle a pinch of salt and pepper over the oil. Set upside down on a foil covered baking sheet with the cleaned inside portion up.
4. In 1 tablespoon coconut oil, sauté diced mushroom stems, zucchini, onion, garlic and tomato.
5. Cook over medium low heat for 4 minutes. Onions will get soft.
6. Take off heat. Add bread crumbs, 2 teaspoons coconut oil and parsley. Mix well. Divide mixture in half.
7. Stuff each mushroom cap with half of the veggie mixture.
8. Bake for 30 minutes in 400° oven uncovered.

VEGETARIAN

CURRY SWEET POTATO WEDGES

Super easy to make and full of finger licking flavor. I usually cut my sweet potatoes into wedges because it is faster prep and the guests can pick up two or 3 for their snack. Much easier than making them into long fries.

SERVES 12; PREP: 15; COOK: 25

Ingredients

- 9 medium sweet potatoes, cut lengthwise into ¼" wedges
- 5 tablespoons coconut oil
- 4 teaspoons curry
- 2 teaspoons smoked paprika
- 3 teaspoons ground ginger
- 1½ teaspoons salt
- freshly ground black pepper

1. Heat oven to 425°
2. Peel the sweet potatoes and cut into wedges.
3. In a large bowl toss potato wedges with melted coconut oil, curry, paprika, ginger, salt, and pepper. Coating each piece well with the spice mixture.
4. Arrange in a single layer on a baking sheet.
5. Cook, turning once, until crisp and browned on all sides, about 20–25 minutes.

FALL VEGETABLE CURRY

Root vegetables, pumpkin and curry are a great fall mix. I add a touch of cinnamon to mine just to keep it interesting. Comfort food at its best. You can make it and serve it as in bowls or serve it over rice or quinoa. This dish is even better the next day when the flavors melt together beautifully. A quick and easy meal to make.

SERVES 4; PREP 15; COOK 15

Ingredients
- 2 teaspoons coconut oil
- 1 cup garbanzo beans
- 1 cup sweet potato, peeled and diced
- 1 cup sweet pumpkin, peeled and diced
- 1 cup parsnip root, peeled and diced
- 1 cup green beans, cut into one inch pieces
- 1 cup vegetable stock
- ½ yellow onion, thinly sliced
- 1 tablespoon madras curry powder blend
- ¼ teaspoon cinnamon
- ¼ teaspoon red pepper flakes
- ½ teaspoon salt
- fresh cilantro for garnish

1. In a large pot, heat the coconut oil over medium heat.
2. Add the onion, potato, pumpkin and parsnip and sauté for 2-3 minutes.
3. Add the rest of the ingredients and bring up to a boil.
4. Lower heat to simmer for 10-15 minutes until veggies are tender.
5. Optional to add a can of fire roasted chopped tomatoes.
6. Grilled Artichoke with Lemon Aioli

GRILLED ARTICHOKE WITH LEMON AIOLI

I love grilled artichokes with a nice dip. It is so easy to make and has a very nice wow factor when served as an appetizer.

Ingredients
- 6 artichokes
- ½ cup good olive oil
- 3 tablespoons chopped parsley
- 1 tablespoon paprika
- 2 teaspoons salt

Easy Lemon Aioli Dip
- 2 cups good mayo
- 3 lemons, juiced and zested

1. Cook the artichokes: Steam bottom sides up until fork tender or you can easily pull a leaf out about 15-20 minutes.
2. Set aside to cool.
3. Once cool, cut the tops off of the artichokes and then cut in half lengthwise.
4. Using a spoon scrape out the thorns and thistles from the inside. May be done one day ahead. Put into fridge and chill.
5. Heat a BBQ up over medium high heat.
6. Using a pastry brush, brush olive oil over the inside and outside of the artichoke including the stem.
7. Sprinkle both sides with salt and paprika.
8. Cook over medium high heat to get a good char on both sides.
9. Put onto platter and sprinkle with chopped parsley.

Quick Lemon Aioli: Mix the juice of the lemons, the zest from the lemons into the good mayo. It will be a bit watery. Put into a container with a lid and put into fridge for 2 hours to set up.

HEMP SEED PESTO

I wanting to create a new pesto recipe and having learned about how much protein and nutrients are in hemp seeds, I thought I would experiment with using hemp seeds in pesto. After a few tries I found the perfect combination of ingredients and did not even miss the parmesan cheese like I thought I would. This easy pesto lasts up to a week in the fridge in a sealed jar.

SERVES 4-6; PREP 10; COOKS

Ingredients
- 1 cup Basil leaves, washed and spun dry
- ¼ cup Extra Virgin Olive Oil
- 1 clove garlic minced
- ½ cup Hulled Hemp Seed

1. Combine basil, garlic, and olive oil in a blender or food processor and blend to preferred texture
2. Add hemp seed and blend just until mixed.
3. Serve immediately or store in a covered container for up to a week.

VEGETARIAN

LAYERED RATATOUILLE

Ratatouille is a traditional French Provencal stewed vegetable dish. There are two good ways to make it. One way is to slice all the veggies and then place them in layers with fresh herbs and bake it. Then you can slice it and see the different layers and colors. The second way is much simpler. Cut up the vegetables in to chunks and simmer on the stove so that all the flavors meld together. I make it both ways. When I bake it, I serve the veggie slices with a side of greens or salad. When I simmer it I will serve it over warm polenta or eat it on its own. It is your choice how you want to make it, both delicious!

SERVES 4-6; PREP 15; COOK 50 MIN

Ingredients

- ½ yellow onion, finely diced
- 3 garlic cloves, finely minced
- 1 zucchini
- 1 yellow squash
- 1 red bell pepper
- 1 small eggplant
- 1 cup tomato puree
- 2 tablespoons olive oil
- ½ teaspoon oregano
- ¼ teaspoon crushed red pepper flakes
- ½ teaspoon salt
- fresh black pepper
- ½ teaspoon fresh thyme leaves

1. Use a mandolin or sharp knife and thinly slice the eggplant, zucchini, squash and bell pepper into slices keeping them in separate piles.
2. Mix the tomato puree, garlic, onion, salt, pepper, oregano and crushed red pepper flakes together. Pour into a baking dish.
3. Layer the veggie slices on top of the tomato sauce alternating veggies from the outer edge in a circle working your way into the inner portion of the spiral.
4. Drizzle the olive oil over the veggies and then sprinkle with salt and pepper. Sprinkle the fresh thyme leaves over the top of the dish.

Continued ➜

LAYERED RATATOUILLE *Continued*

5. Cover the dish and bake for 50 minutes.
6. When you remove the dish from the oven and uncover, you will see that the veggies released some of their liquid and that the tomato sauce has bubbled up around them.
7. Let the dish set for 5-10 minutes before serving.
8. Serve warm or at room temperature.

VEGETARIAN

LEMON CAULIFLOWER

This is a great tasty appetizer that is crunchy, tender and full of lemon flavor. Make a big batch and stick some toothpicks in and watch it get gobbled up. Very good room temperature so you can make this ahead.

SERVES 10; PREP: 10; COOK: 15

Ingredients

- 1 head cauliflower (about 2 pounds), cored and cut into 1" florets
- Zest of two lemons
- Juice of two lemons
- 1 teaspoon turmeric
- 1 teaspoon cayenne
- 1 teaspoon salt
- freshly ground black pepper
- 3 tablespoons coconut oil

1. Bring a large pot of salted water to a boil; add cauliflower and cook until just tender, about 5 minutes.
2. Transfer to an ice bath until chilled; drain and dry completely with kitchen towels.
3. Sprinkle the cauliflower with the lemon zest, turmeric, cayenne, salt and pepper.
4. Heat coconut oil in a skillet.
5. Cooking in batches over medium high heat, brown the cauliflower.
6. Plate and sprinkle lemon juice over.

LENTILS AND RICE (MUJADRAH)

This Middle Eastern lentils and rice dish called Mujadrah is something quite special. I grew up in Mexico and Central America when I was young and am familiar with rice and beans, this dish is not that! I think it is the mix of the cumin, allspice, cinnamon and mint that makes my taste buds dance. The first time I had it I could not get enough. I kept going back week after week to order a take out order of it. Once I discovered how simple it is to make, it has become one of my favorite go to meals.

SERVES 4; PREP 10; COOK 40-50 MINUTES

Ingredients

- ½ cup lentils
- ½ cup brown basmati rice or long grain brown rice
- 2 cups vegetable broth
- ½ yellow onion, diced
- 1 teaspoon coconut oil
- 4 cloves of garlic, minced
- 1½ teaspoons cumin
- ½ teaspoon allspice
- ½ teaspoon cinnamon
- ⅓ cup mint leaves, thinly sliced into ribbons

1. Heat a medium pot that has a lid over medium high heat.
2. Add the oil and let it melt and then add the onion and garlic. Stirring as it cooks 2-3 minutes until the onion is translucent, do not burn the garlic.
3. Add the cumin, allspice and cinnamon, stir it into the onion mixture for about half a minute.
4. Add the vegetable broth, rice and lentils, stir.
5. Cover and bring to boil and then reduce heat to a simmer and let cook 40 minutes without taking off the lid.
6. If there is still some broth, cook another 5 minutes until broth is absorbed.
7. Let stand off of heat for 10 minutes.
8. Then stir in the mint, reserving half for garnish, into the rice and lentil mixture.
9. Serve while it is warm.

MOROCCAN INSPIRED VEGGIE CHICKPEA SOUP

This Moroccan inspired Veggie Chick Pea Soup is a meal in a bowl. It is a hearty dish and with a nice green salad makes a nice full meal. I have to say I get on kicks where this is all I want to eat because it is that good. I always have New Mexican Roasted Green Chilies in my freezer and they work so well with the curry paste and coconut milk. It is just a bowl of heaven. The sweet potato and apple adds a sweetness that is delightful.

SERVES 4; PREP 15; COOK 30-40

Ingredients

- 1 can of unsweetened coconut milk
- 1 sweet potato, peeled and diced
- 1 apple, peeled and diced
- 1 can of chick peas, rinsed and drained
- 1 can of fire roasted tomatoes
- ½ cup or 2 cans of fire roasted green chilies
- 1 bell pepper, seeded, deveined and diced
- 1 large carrot, peeled and diced
- 3 cups veggie stock
- 3 cloves garlic, minced
- 2 limes, divided
- ½ head cilantro, chopped
- 1 tablespoon red curry paste
- ¼ teaspoon cinnamon
- ¼ teaspoon cumin
- ½ teaspoon salt

1. Put all the coconut milk, lime and curry paste in a soup pot and bring up to heat while the curry paste melts into the coconut milk.
2. Add the juice of one lime and all the other ingredients except the cilantro to the pot and stir well.
3. Bring up to a boil and then lower to a simmer and cook until the veggies are tender, 30-40 minutes.
4. Serve with sprinkled cilantro on top of the soup bowls and a wedge of lime .

QUINOA ENCHILADA BAKE

I love enchiladas and have not made them as often since I went dairy free. I think the big goops of melty cheese as the star at the time. Yet, when I made this recipe, I never missed the cheese or the tortillas. It creates warm yummy bowls of goodness. I added the cashew cream to add a touch of richness and also to thicken it.

I was amazed at how much the quinoa expanded in the crock pot! I had almost used 2 cups but there would not have been enough room. This dish would also be good with shredded chicken but I did not miss the meat.

It is a great meal that cooks itself, very budget friendly and it can feed a crowd. I am thinking a perfect dish for a pot luck or a Sunday game day!

PREP: 10; COOK: 3.5 - 4 HOURS; SERVES 4-6

Ingredients

- 1 cup quinoa, uncooked
- 1 can fire roasted tomatoes
- 2 cups enchilada sauce
- 1 chopped green chiles, drained
- 1 cup corn kernels
- 1 can black beans, drained and rinsed
- ½ cup water
- ½ cup tomato sauce
- 2 tablespoons chopped fresh cilantro leaves
- 1 teaspoon cumin
- ½ teaspoon chili powder
- ½ cup cashew cream (optional)
- 1 avocado, halved, seeded, peeled and diced
- Chopped cilantro for garnish

1. Put all the ingredients except for the avocado and cilantro into a crock pot and mix well.
2. Cover and cook on low for 3.5 to 4 hours, stirring a few times.
3. Serve with avocado and cilantro.

VEGETARIAN

QUINOA ROOT VEGGIE STUFFED CABBAGE

I loved traditional stuffed cabbage but decided to try it with quinoa instead of rice and root veggies instead of meat and it turned out fantastic. The sweetness of the root veggies called for some cinnamon that just makes this dish pop. I put sweet potato, butternut squash, parsnip and apple inside these lovely cabbage leaves. I have used purple, green and Napa cabbage as my wraps and found them all to be excellent. You could even use collard leaves if you wanted to.

Serves 4; Prep 15; Cook 90 minutes

Ingredients

For the Filling:
- 1 head of cabbage
- 1 sweet potato, peeled and diced
- 1 cup butternut squash, diced
- 1 large parsnip, peeled and diced
- 1 onion, cut into chunks (purple or yellow)
- 1 apple, peeled, cored, diced
- ½ cup yellow raisins, soaked 10 min in hot water
- 4 cloves garlic, minced
- 1 teaspoon cinnamon
- ½ teaspoon nutmeg
- ½ teaspoon salt
- fresh black pepper
- 2 tablespoon olive oil
- 2 cups cooked quinoa

For the Sauce:
- 1 can crushed tomatoes
- 1 carrot, grated finely
- 3 cloves garlic, minced
- ½ yellow onion, grated
- ½ teaspoon cinnamon
- ¼ teaspoon nutmeg
- ¼ teaspoon allspice
- ½ teaspoon salt
- fresh ground pepper

1. Pre heat oven to 375 degrees F
2. Bring a large stockpot filled with water to a boil.

Continued ➜

QUINOA ROOT VEGGIE STUFFED CABBAGE *Continued*

3. Cut the core out of the head of cabbage and drop into the boiling water, cook for 5-7 minutes until it gets soft. Remove and set aside to cool.
4. Take all the ingredients for the filling except the quinoa and raisins and mix together well in a large bowl. Then pour onto a sheet pan and roast in the oven until they get soft and start to brown, about 50 minutes.
5. To make the sauce while the veggies roast, combine all the ingredients in a sauce pan and bring up to boil and then lower to low heat and simmer while the veggies cook.
6. Ladle about ⅓ of the sauce into a casserole dish.
7. Mix the roast veggies, raisins and quinoa in a large bowl.
8. Peel the cabbage leaves off of the head of cabbage gently making a pile.
9. Put some of the veggie mix in the cabbage leaf and tuck in the ends and roll up like a burrito. Place in baking dish seam side done.
10. Do this until all the stuffing has been rolled up. Pour the remainder of the sauce over the cabbage rolls.
11. Bake in the oven for 30 minutes.
12. This is a great dish to make ahead of time, to freeze and you can do the final cooking in a slow cooker if you wish.

VEGETARIAN

SHEPHERD'S PIE

This Shepherds Pie comes from humble beginnings but it is still a favorite comfort food. With the addition of the right seasonings we can take it to another level. This recipe uses mashed cauliflower for the topping. Feel free to substitute mashed butternut squash, mashed acorn squash or mashed sweet potato.

SERVES 6-8; PREP 15; COOK 45

Ingredients

- 1 Tbs coconut oil
- 4-6 cloves garlic, chopped
- 3 lb. ground beef
- 2 cups onions, chopped
- 2 cups carrots, chopped
- 2 stalks celery, chopped
- 1 tablespoon fresh rosemary, chopped
- 3 teaspoons fresh thyme, chopped
- 6 oz tomato paste
- 2 Tbs balsamic vinegar
- 6 c mashed cauliflower

1. Preheat the oven to 350.
2. Heat large frying pan over medium heat. Once hot, add ground beef, cooking until browned.
3. While browning mince garlic and dice onion, carrots and celery.
4. Drain the juices from ground beef and set aside.
5. Set pan on medium heat again and add oil. Once oil is hot, add onions, garlic, carrots and celery to pan on medium heat. Sauté until onion is translucent and carrot and celery are tender. Add rosemary and thyme.
6. Add browned ground beef back into pan and combine with balsamic, tomato paste and mix well.
7. Pour into baking dish and cover with mashed cauliflower.
8. Bake for 45 minutes until cauliflower begins to have areas of light golden brown.

Note: This may be made a day a head, covered and put into the fridge. If putting in oven from fridge cook for 60-70 minutes.

SPICY INDIAN DAL (LENTILS)

It took me a long time to try this dish but once I tried spicy Indian Dal, I was hooked. You can choose how spicy to make it. It is usually served over rice. This recipe may have two seasonings you might not have, but they are worth the purchase since they can be used in so many other recipes. They are mustard seeds and ground coriander seed. This is an easy dish to make and has tons of flavor.

SERVES 4; PREP 10 MIN; COOK 25 - 30 MINUTES

Ingredients

- 1 cup red or orange lentils
- 4 cups of water divided
- 2 tablespoons fresh ginger root, minced
- 4 tomatoes, diced
- 2 yellow onions, diced
- 2-3 jalapeño peppers, deveined, seeded and minced
- 5 cloves of garlic, minced
- 2 tablespoons coconut oil
- 2 teaspoons mustard seeds
- 1 tablespoon ground cumin
- 1 tablespoon ground coriander seed
- ½ teaspoon salt
- 3 tablespoons fresh cilantro, chopped

1. In a pot add 2 cups of the water and the lentils, bring up to boil and then turn down to medium low for 25-30 minutes until soft.
2. While the lentils are cooking, heat the coconut oil in a skillet over medium high heat.
3. Add the mustard seeds and when they begin to move around the pan, add the onions, ginger, jalapeño peppers and garlic.
4. Stir and salute until the onions are golden brown about 6-8 minutes. Don't walk away from the pan, you do not want the onions or garlic to burn.
5. Add the cumin, coriander and tomatoes stirring well and cooking until the tomatoes are cooked and falling apart.

6. Add one cup of water and bring up to a low boil for 5 minutes.
7. Drain the cooked lentils and add to the boiling mixture, stir. Add the salt and the cilantro.
8. Remove from heat and serve while warm. If you have to wait do not add the cilantro, keep covered to keep warm and add the cilantro right before serving.

STUFFED EGGPLANT

This stuffed eggplant comes alive with the brininess of the olives, sweetness of the raisins and flavor of the garlic. All of the veggies cook together nicely with the tender eggplant containers. Perfect for a week night dinner or even for company. Each guest receiving a stuffed half of eggplant with a side of greens for a perfect plate.

SERVES 2; PREP 10; COOK 45

Ingredients
- 1 large eggplant
- ½ bell pepper, diced
- ½ yellow onion, diced
- 3 cloves garlic, minced
- ¼ cup golden raisins, soaked in warm water 10 minutes
- 1 medium tomato, diced
- 2 tablespoons green olives, pitted and diced
- 1 tablespoon olive oil
- ¼ teaspoon salt
- fresh black pepper

1. Pre heat oven to 375 degrees F
2. Cut the tops off the eggplant and slice in half lengthwise.
3. Scoop our the inside so that about ¼ inch of the flesh is left.
4. Rub the olive oil on the inside and outside of the eggplant halves. Place open side up in a baking pan.
5. Chop the scooped out portion of the eggplant and put into a bowl.
6. Add the bell pepper, onion, garlic, the soaked and drained raisins, tomato, olives, salt and pepper and stir together.
7. Put the veggie mix inside of the eggplant and cover the dish.
8. Bake for 45 minutes.

VEGETARIAN

STUFFED POBLANO PEPPER

This stuffed poblano pepper is not your ordinary stuffed bell pepper. The poblano pepper is a bit spicy which makes the dish full of flavor. It is then stuffed with black beans, potatoes, tomato, onion, garlic and lots of great flavor. For a more tender pepper, drop the whole pepper into a pot of boiling water for 3-4 minutes, remove and drop in ice water to shock it and stop the cooking. Personally I like to put it in the oven and let it cook, it has a little more texture and holds the stuffing better.

Whether you slice the pepper in half to fill it or you cut the top off and stuff it, it is a fantastic way to have an easy delicious dinner. Great for company too with a nice side salad of shredded romaine lettuce, chopped cilantro and lime juice.

SERVES 1; PREP 15; COOK 35

Ingredients

- 1 poblano pepper
- 2 tablespoons onion
- 1 roma tomato
- 1 garlic clove
- ½ cup black beans
- 1-teaspoon coconut oil
- ¼ teaspoon chili powder
- ¼ teaspoon cumin
- ½ cup Yukon gold potatoes (1 medium potato)
- ½ cup and 2 tablespoons vegan pepper jack cheese (optional)
- ⅛ – ¼ teaspoon salt

1. Preheat oven to 400 degrees F
2. Seed and chop the tomato.
3. Dice the onion and the potato.
4. Grate the cheese and rinse the beans.
5. Sauté the onion, garlic, and potato in the coconut oil over medium heat.

Continued ➔

STUFFED POBLANO PEPPER *Continued*

6. Cook 5 minutes. The potatoes will be tender and the onions translucent.
7. In a bowl, add the sauté mixture, black beans, tomato, chili powder and cumin. Mix well. Add salt to taste, 1/8–1/4 teaspoon.
8. Mix 1/2 cup of the cheese in.
9. Cut a rectangle in the pepper, removing the piece.
10. Cut out the membranes and seeds keeping the pepper intact.
11. Place pepper into a small baking dish.
12. Gently stuff the pepper with the mixture stretching the side's open and having a mound in the center. The entire pepper should be stuffed with the mixture.
13. Pat the 2 tablespoons of cheese over the exposed stuffing.
14. Bake 400° for 35 minutes. Cheese will begin to brown on the top.

VEGETARIAN

SWEET POTATO ENCHILADAS

PREP 15; COOK 30; SERVES 4

Ingredients
- 2 sweet potatoes
- 1 can black beans
- 1 can green chilies (or 3 roasted and peeled ones)
- 1 red bell pepper diced
- 1 small yellow onion diced
- 2 garlic cloves minced
- 2 cups green salsa
- 12 corn tortillas
- 4 tbl chopped cilantro
- 1 tea chili powder
- 1 teaspoon cumin
- ½ tea salt
- ¼ tea black pepper
- 1 bag of vegan shredded cheddar cheese (2cups)

1. Pre heat oven 350 degrees
2. Peel and dice the sweet potatoes. Put in a sauce pot cover with cold water and bring to a boil. Cook until sweet potatoes are tender and a fork can pierce easily about 12 minutes.
3. Drain and rinse the black beans or use 1½ cups of home made black beans. Place in a large bowl.
4. Add the cooked sweet potatoes, green chilies, diced onions, minced garlic, diced bell pepper, cilantro, chili powder, cumin, salt and pepper. Mix well.
5. Put enough salsa to cover the 9 x 13 inch baking dish. Heat up the tortillas. Put 3 table spoons of sweet potato mix in the center of the tortilla and sprinkle with a table spoon of the vegan cheddar cheese. Roll the tortilla and put seam side down in the baking dish. Repeat with the rest of the tortillas filling each one, rolling and laying it in bottom of baking dish next to the prior one. Repeat until done.
6. Pour remaining salsa over the enchiladas and sprinkle with 1 cup of the remaining cheese. Bake for 30 minutes until done.
7. Serve hot.
8. Garnish with chopped cilantro or tomato.

THAI INSPIRED ALMOND NUT SAUCE

I love a good peanut sauce with my chicken satays when I go out for Thai food. I have discovered something better, this sauce! I use this sauce on my Thai Chicken Satays that I put into butter lettuce leafs. I also use this when I make Thai Fresh Spring Rolls. It is a sauce that can drizzle nicely over the goodies in the lettuce leaves and has a bit of a bite.

PREP: 15; COOL: 0; SERVES: 3

Ingredients

- ½ cup almond nut butter
- ½ cup unsweetened coconut milk
- 1¼ teaspoon rice vinegar
- 2 tablespoons tamari
- ½ teaspoon crushed red pepper flakes
- ½ teaspoon fresh grated ginger or 1 teaspoon ground ginger
- 3 tablespoons fresh lime juice
- ¼ teaspoon cayenne pepper

1. Put all the ingredients into a blender and blend well.
2. This can be done in a food processor also.
3. If you want thiner consistency add more coconut milk.

VEGAN ALFREDO SAUCE

Giving up dairy does not have to mean giving up Alfredo sauce. Now and then I get a craving for a good Alfredo sauce and this is the recipe I turn to now that I am dairy free. In fact, your dinner guests might actually be shocked to learn that there is no dairy in this sauce. I added a touch of garlic to the sauce, feel free to add a few more cloves if you really want the garlic flavor.

I have found this sauce to work well over zucchini noodles, spaghetti noodles and gluten free noodles. Roast chicken or sautéed prawns are tasty in this sauce also.

PREP: 10; COOK: 10; SERVES: 4

Ingredients
- ½ cup raw whole cashews, soak for 4 hours in water
- 1 cup vegetable stock
- 1 yellow onion, finely chopped
- ½ teaspoon salt
- ½ teaspoon ground black pepper
- 2 large garlic cloves, minced
- 1 tablespoon lemon juice
- ¼ cup nutritional yeast
- 1 tablespoon coconut oil

1. In a medium skillet, heat the coconut oil over medium heat.
2. Add the finely minced onion and sauté over medium low heat. Once the onions become translucent, about 5 minutes, add the finely minced garlic. Continue to cook for 3 minutes, stirring so that nothing burns.
3. In a high speed blender add the cooked onion and garlic.
4. Drain and rinse the cashew after they soak.
5. Add the cashews, stock, lemon juice, nutritional yeast, salt and pepper to the onion/garlic mixture.
6. Blend on high until smooth and creamy.
7. Pour sauce in a medium skillet and heat up. Then serve over your desired noodles: zucchini noodles, rice noodles or gluten free noodles.

VEGETARIAN CHILI

Vegetarian chili never sounded exciting to me until I made it myself. I wanted chili and had a ton of produce to use. I grew up eating a hot bowl of beef chili after a day of skiing in the mountains of New Mexico. I use to love to ski; it made me feel so free. I would ski even if there were a huge snowstorm.

I loved coming home to a bowl of homemade chili that had been cooking all day. The house would smell incredible. I have created a very hearty chili with similar flavors based on those memories. I may not ski anymore, but I love the smell of the house as the chili cooks and the robust flavors it has. The nice thing is that this is an easy recipe and it cooks quickly.

PREP TIME: 15 MINUTES ; COOK TIME: 30 MINUTES; SERVES: 4

- 2 tablespoons coconut oil
- 1 yellow onion diced
- 5 cloves garlic minced
- 1 sweet potato diced
- 4 tomatos diced
- 1 red bell pepper diced
- 1 yellow bell pepper diced
- 1 zucchini diced
- 1 cup corn kernels
- 1½ teaspoons cumin
- 6 teaspoons chili powder
- 1½ cups water
- ¾ teaspoon salt
- 1 15 ounce can black beans drained
- ½ 15 ounce can garbanzo beans drained
- ½ 15 ounce can kidney beans
- 1 8 ounce can tomato sauce
- 4 tablespoons chopped chives

VEGETARIAN

WARM HERB OLIVES

Dice the vegetables into the same size of the pinto beans so that everything cooks evenly.

Sauté the onion and garlic in the olive oil for 3 minutes so that the onion gets translucent.

Add the rest of the diced vegetables and sauté for 2 minutes.

Add the beans, tomato sauce, water, chili powder, cumin and salt. Stir well. Cover and cook over low heat for 25 minutes stirring occasionally.

I like to use a mix of pitted and not pitted olives and a mix of types in this dish. The warm olives with garlic, lemon and rosemary is always a hit.

SERVES: 12; PREP: 10; COOK: 12

- ½cup extra-virgin olive oil
- zest of 2 lemons
- 2small rosemary sprigs
- 5 garlic cloves, thickly sliced
- 6 cups of mixed oil- and brine-cured olives (Kalamata, Niçoise, Moroccan, cracked green Sicilian and Cerignola)

1. In a medium saucepan, combine the oil with the lemon zest, rosemary sprigs and garlic.
2. Cook over low heat until the garlic just begins to brown, 10-12 minutes. This will infuse the olive oil with flavor.
3. Remove from the heat, stir in the olives and let stand covered for at least 15 minutes before serving so they soak up the flavor.

Made in the USA
Las Vegas, NV
09 June 2021